# *Simply*

# *1-2-3*

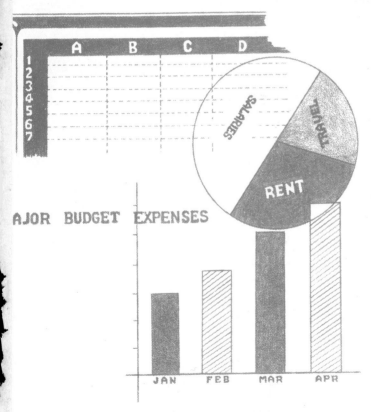

AJOR BUDGET EXPENSES

*Mary Campbell*

Osborne McGraw-Hill
2600 Tenth Street
Berkeley, California 94710
U.S.A.

Osborne McGraw-Hill offers software for sale. For information on software, translations, or book distributors outside of the U.S.A., please write to Osborne McGraw-Hill at the above address.

*Simply 1-2-3*

1234567890 DOC 9987654321

ISBN 0-07-881751-X

# Acknowledgments

I would like to thank the many individuals who gave so much of their time and talent to help shape this book:

Gabrielle Lawrence for her work on all aspects of the project. Her creative ideas helped make the artwork and illustrations easy to understand.

Kenna Wood and Allen Wyatt for their idea to do this *Simply...* series. Their perceptive look at the marketplace allowed them to realize that many users need a quick way to get at the essentials of a software package, with only a minimal time investment.

Liz Fisher for reading the manuscript and helping to fine-tune its contents for our audience.

Wendy Goss for double-checking the chapters as they came in, making sure every chapter was complete.

Carol Henry for her developmental edit and copyedit, helping this to be a book that makes learning 1-2-3 easy for anyone.

Susie Kim for her wonderful rendering of the artwork ideas. Susie's work makes this an inviting book that clearly illustrates 1-2-3's main features.

*Mary Campbell*

**Publisher**
Kenna S. Wood

**Acquisitions Editor**
Elizabeth Fisher

**Associate Editor**
Wendy Goss

**Project Editor**
Madhu Prasher

**Developmental and Copy Editor**
Carol Henry

**Proofreading Coordinator**
Erica Spaberg

**Proofreaders**
Elizabeth von Radics, Colleen Paretty

**Indexer**
Valerie Robbins

**Illustrator**
Susie C. Kim

**Cover Design**
Mason Fong
Patricia A. Mon

**Computer Designers**
Marcela Hancik
J. E. Christgau
Michelle Salinaro
Helena Charm
Patricia Jani Beckwith
Peter Hancik
Fred Lass
Lance Ravella
Stefany Otis

# Contents

# It's Simple to Use This Lay-Flat Binding...

Open this book to any page you choose and crease back the left-hand page by pressing along the length of the spine with your fingers. Now, the book will stay open until you're ready to go on to another page.

Unlike regular book bindings, this special binding won't weaken or crack when you crease back the pages. It's tough, durable, and resilient—designed to withstand years of daily use. So go ahead, put this book to the test and use it as often as you like.

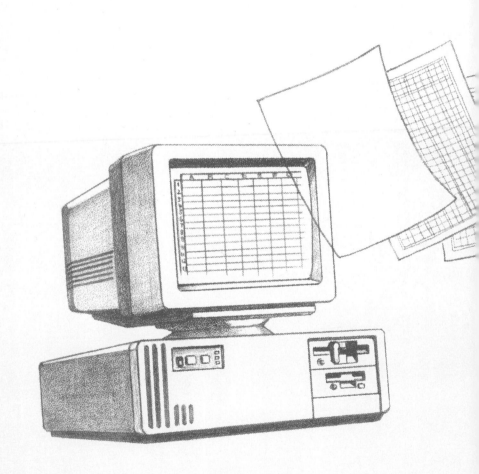

# *Starting and Ending a 1-2-3 Session*

1-2-3 is a computer program that provides a large electronic sheet of paper on your computer screen. This electronic paper, called a *spreadsheet* or *worksheet*, is like a large sheet of ledger paper. It is ideal for performing all types of calculations.

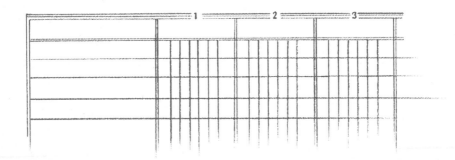

Although you may not have used ledger paper for your calculations, you have probably seen it. It is usually green or yellow and is always arranged in rows and columns to make it easy to organize your data as you enter it. It might make you think of an accountant with a green eyeshade, but individuals in all professions and walks of life use

ledger paper because it helps to organize numeric information.

1-2-3's electronic worksheet shares the structure of ledger paper, yet it provides a much larger work area than any piece of ledger paper sold. 1-2-3 also offers many features not available on a regular sheet of ledger paper, such as the ability to automatically add commas or dollar signs to your numeric entries.

1-2-3 is ideally suited for recording budgets, sales figures, and payroll data. In these situations, or *applications*, the same calculations must be performed repetitively, yet the numbers used in the calculations will be new each time. Once you record the computations and formulas, all you need to do is type new numbers for updated results. You can enter any type of data that you wish, and the more your data changes, the more time 1-2-3 saves over paper methods.

COMMISSION CALCULATIONS

1992 BUDGET

| | SALES | COMMISSION |
|---|---|---|
| Bob Smith | 169,500 | $2,000 |
| Jon Doe | 215,000 | $2,500 |
| Joe Blow | 113,500 | —o— |
| Don Davis | 143,000 | |

| | 1990 | 1991 | 1992 PROJECTED |
|---|---|---|---|
| Travel | 1560 | 2125 | 2700 |
| Rent | 750 | 900 | |
| Utilities | 2075 | 2690 | |
| Auto | 560 | | |

SALES PROJECTS

| 1991 | 35 |
|---|---|
| 1992 | 41 |
| 1993 | 37 |
| 1994 | 34 |

| | 1991 | 1992 |
|---|---|---|
| BOATS | 150,000 | 110,000 |
| AUTO | 675,000 | 720,000 |
| TRAINS | 295,000 | 315,000 |

# Getting Ready to Use 1-2-3

Before you can use 1-2-3, you have some preparations to handle. The first step is ensuring that DOS and 1-2-3 are installed on your computer. DOS is an *operating system* that allows 1-2-3 and other products to communicate with the *hardware*. Hardware is your equipment—all the physical computer components that you purchased. These include a system unit (processor), a monitor, and perhaps a printer.

DOS is installed when you receive the machine, or you may need to install it, following the instructions that accompany it. In Appendix A of this book, you will find complete instructions for installing 1-2-3 on your machine, if this has not yet been done.

The second step you need to take is turning on your system and loading the operating system. This process is called *booting* your system. You will need to know a few things about your computer hardware before beginning this procedure.

Every system has at least one *disk drive*. Your system may have a floppy disk drive, a hard disk drive, or both. Floppy disk drives are easily identified because you can see the slot where the removable floppy disk is placed in the drive. Hard disks are usually hidden inside the computer.

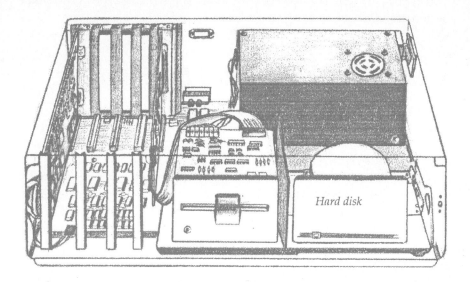

Hard disk

You will need to know if there is a hard disk in your system unit, because the procedure for booting your system is different if you have a hard disk. Also, later releases of 1-2-3 require a hard disk and cannot be used unless you have one. If you have a hard disk in your computer, check the floppy disk drives and take out any disks that are there. If your system does not have a hard disk, you must put a DOS disk in the system drive (drive A), which is the top one or the one on the left.

Next, turn your system on. Your system will boot up and load DOS when you turn on the processor. You may need to press as many as four switches to be sure that each component is on. The processor and monitor will each have an On switch. If you have a printer, it will use a separate switch. Likewise, any external drives that may be attached to your system will also have an On switch.

*Software* consists of programs—instructions that make your equipment perform the tasks that you want. (Your DOS operating system is software.) Normally software comes in a box that contains several disks and a manual.

The box that contains your 1-2-3 software indicates the release of 1-2-3 that you are buying. The box also contains information on the type of computer system that is required to run the release.

# Changing to the 1-2-3 Directory

*Note: If you do not have a hard disk, you can start 1-2-3 directly from the 1-2-3 System disk that you will place in the system drive A, and you can skip to the beginning of the next section, "Starting Your 1-2-3 Session."*

Now that your system is on, before you can start 1-2-3 you will need to activate the *file lists* that contain the hard disk files needed by 1-2-3. File lists that help organize a hard disk are called *directories*. A directory is nothing more than a list of files that might look something like this:

If when you installed 1-2-3 you used the directory name that Lotus suggested in the installation program, you will be able to determine the name of the directory where the 1-2-3 files are located based on the release of 1-2-3 that you have on your

```
Volume in drive C has no label
Volume Serial Number is 159C-5E8E
Directory of C:\BUDGET

.              <DIR>       08-30-91    4:30p
..             <DIR>       08-30-91    4:30p
TRAVEL   WK1       115824  09-26-91   12:04p
SALES    WK1       194456  09-26-91   12:06p
SALARY   WK1       112646  09-26-91   12:08p
BLDG     WK1          294  10-06-91    3:14p
MISC     WK1         1983  10-06-91    3:14p
        7 File(s)      424483  bytes
                     24246272  bytes free
```

system. For instance, with 1-2-3 Release 2.3, the directory suggested is 123R23. You can activate this directory by typing **CD \123R23**. (CD is the DOS command for Change Directory.)

Determine which version of 1-2-3 you are using, and then type **CD \** followed by the directory name that matches your release, as shown here:

| Release No. | Command |
|---|---|
| Release 1A | CD \123 |
| Release 2.01 | CD \123 |
| Release 2.2 | CD \123R22 |
| Release 2.3 | CD \123R23 |
| Release 3.0 | CD \123R3 |
| Release 3.1 | CD \123R31 |

## Starting Your 1-2-3 Session

If you are using a hard disk, once the 1-2-3 directory is active, all you need to do to start the 1-2-3 program is type **123** and press ENTER. If you do not have a hard disk, place your 1-2-3 System disk in drive A; then type **123** and press ENTER to begin. 1-2-3 displays an introductory screen, and then another screen where you will do your work with 1-2-3. This screen represents the top-left corner of your 1-2-3 worksheet.

## Ending a 1-2-3 Session

One way of ending your 1-2-3 session is to turn your system off—however, this is not a good approach because 1-2-3 will not close open files or allow you to save any of your work. A better approach is to ask 1-2-3 to end the session. You do this by first making 1-2-3's main menu active by typing a **/**.

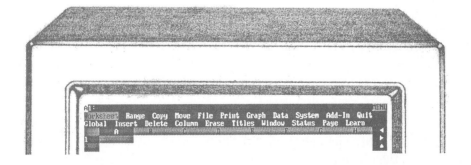

The menu that appears at the top of your screen offers a variety of choices, and the one you need to end the session is Quit. You can choose Quit by typing Q, or by highlighting Quit using the RIGHT or LEFT ARROW key and then pressing ENTER. You will then be asked to confirm your request by typing Y for Yes.

## Keys to Success

To start 1-2-3 you must have the operating system (DOS) in memory. With a hard disk system you must activate the directory that contains the 1-2-3 program files. With a floppy disk system, place the 1-2-3 System disk in drive A.

To start a 1-2-3 session, type **123** and press ENTER.

To end a 1-2-3 session, first type / to activate the main menu, and then type **QY** to select Quit and confirm your command.

## What Do They Mean By . . . ?

Booting    The process of activating the operating system software.

Directory    An organization of files on a disk.

File    A collection of data or program information stored on disk.

Hardware    The physical pieces of computer equipment that you purchased.

Operating System    The software that controls all activities within the computer.

Software    Instructions (programs) that allow the computer to perform a specific task (application).

Control
Panel ➔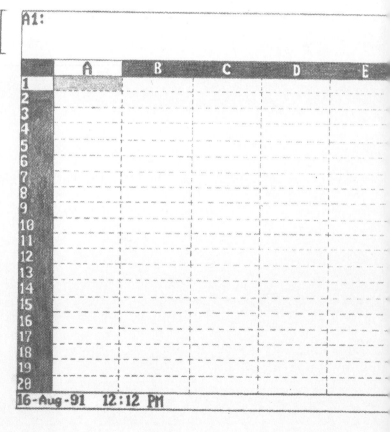

# *Understanding the Worksheet*

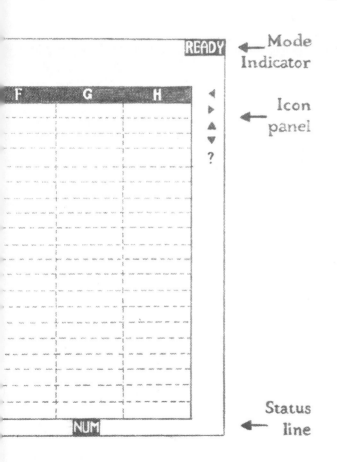

READY ← Mode Indicator

Icon ← panel

Status ← line

The worksheet looks small when you first start 1-2-3, since you are looking only at its upper-left corner. Your computer screen is like a magnifying glass that allows you to take a close-up look at a small section of the worksheet while the rest of it remains out of sight. The worksheet is much larger than what you initially view—there are actually 256 columns and as many as 8192 rows, if you are using one of the more recent releases of 1-2-3.

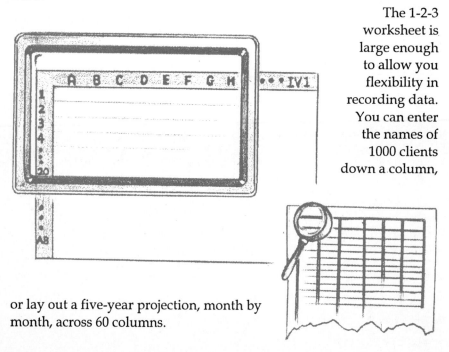

The 1-2-3 worksheet is large enough to allow you flexibility in recording data. You can enter the names of 1000 clients down a column, or lay out a five-year projection, month by month, across 60 columns.

## The Worksheet Structure

Because the worksheet's size is much larger than a single sheet of ledger paper, you can lose your bearings if you don't have a basic understanding of the worksheet structure. 1-2-3's worksheet makes finding your location easy. Each column has a unique identifier, or column name. The first column is column A, the second is column B, and so on until all 26 letters of the alphabet are used. The double letters AA through AZ are used to identify the next 26 columns. These are followed by BA through BZ, and this sequence continues until the last column, which is assigned the double-letter name IV.

The rows on the worksheet are numbered sequentially. The first row is row 1 and the last row is 8192.

The intersection of each row and column in the invisible grid pattern on your screen is called a *cell*. On ledger paper, the lines are there to show the intersection where each entry should be made. Ledger paper often provides an additional vertical line in each column to indicate where decimal places should be entered; this separation is not present in the electronic version.

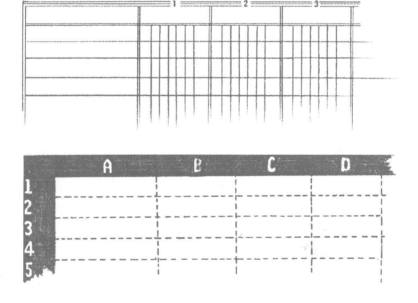

There are millions of cells on 1-2-3's electronic worksheet, but it's easy to uniquely identify each one—by stating the *cell address*. This always consists of the cell's column letter followed by the row number that contains the cell. A1, Z10, DF2000, and IV400 are all examples of valid cell addresses. Anyone familiar with a worksheet will know a location instantly when you tell them the cell address. Specifying a cell address is the same as specifying the address for a house or an apartment. It may be a bit more concise, but the objective is still the same: to indicate an exact location.

# Watching What 1-2-3 Is Doing

When you are driving your car, you look at the dashboard for important indicators such as your driving speed or the engine's temperature. You need to look at these gauges and meters on the dashboard to get current information on the operation of your car. Similarly, when you work with 1-2-3 you also look in special places for this information: the *control panel*, consisting of the top three lines of the screen, and the *status line*, which is the very last line on the screen. Each location provides different types of information critical to staying in sync with what 1-2-3 is trying to accomplish for you.

Although these screen areas are similar in all releases of 1-2-3, there may be some subtle differences between the various releases. The control panel and status line information discussed in this book is the same for all releases.

# The Control Panel

The top three lines of the screen are called the *control panel*. This is the area that you use to indicate your

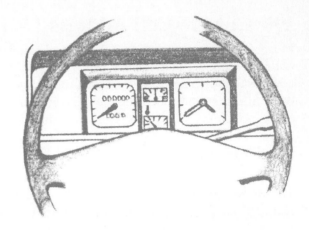

*Control panel* —

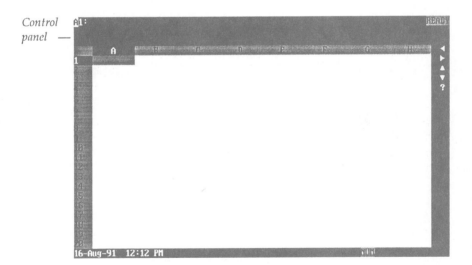

requests to 1-2-3. It is also where 1-2-3 tells you its current state and the contents of the current cell.

## The Current Cell Address

Most of the time, the top line of the control panel displays the current cell address. Since A1 is the active cell when you first start 1-2-3, A1 is the address that displays initially. Later, following the address, you will see other information concerning the cell contents. Since this cell and all the others are empty when you begin, only the address displays.

## The Mode Indicator

The right corner of the top line in the control panel contains a *mode indicator*. This is one of the most important pieces of information on the screen because it tells you what 1-2-3 is currently doing (the *mode*). Initially this mode indicator reads READY. You can think of READY mode as a green light telling you that 1-2-3 is ready to process your next request. Other mode indicators, such as MENU or HELP, indicate that you are selecting options from a menu or accessing help information.

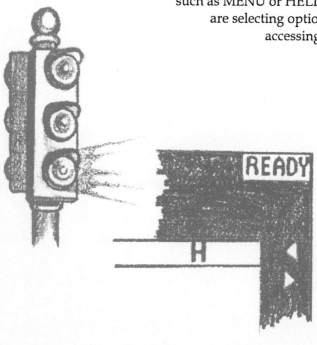

## 1-2-3 Modes

Here are definitions of some of the more common displays you will see in the mode indicator in the upper-right corner of the control panel:

EDIT    1-2-3 will allow you to correct the entry in the current cell without retyping it.

LABEL    1-2-3 is expecting you to complete a text entry in the current cell.

MENU    1-2-3 is waiting for you to make a selection from the menu at the top of the screen.

READY    1-2-3 is not currently performing any action and is ready to process your next request.

VALUE    1-2-3 is expecting you to complete the entry of a number or computation in the current cell.

WAIT    1-2-3 is processing your last request and cannot start a new task until it finishes.

## The Next Two Lines

The remaining lines in the control panel will become significant as you begin to make entries on the worksheet. The contents of these lines will be discussed at that time.

# The Status Line

Many releases of 1-2-3 always display the date and time at the left end of the *status line* at the bottom of the screen. Although this lets you see the current settings for the date and time in your computer, it is the least important piece of information in the status line.

When it has something else to tell you, 1-2-3 overlays the date/time display with more important information, such as error messages. For example, attempting to use a printer that is not ready or a floppy disk drive that is empty will cause an error message to display in the status line. Error messages remain until you press the key labeled Esc (Escape) to acknowledge that you have seen the message. In Release 2.3, many error messages appear in a box superimposed on the middle of the screen.

Sometimes the status line indicates that certain keys have been pressed. For example, if the Caps Lock key is pressed to lock the alphabetic keys (for typing all capital letters), CAPS appears on the status line. Pressing Caps Lock a second time disengages the all-caps feature and removes the CAPS indicator from the status line.

*Tip: When Caps Lock is not engaged, you must use the Shift key when you wish to type capital letters. Note that to type the special symbols at the top of keys, you must always use the Shift key; Caps Lock has no effect on these keys.*

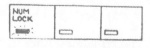

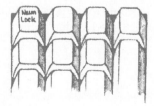

If you press the Num Lock key to engage the numeric keypad (to type only numbers), NUM appears in the status line. To disengage the numeric keypad so you can again use directional arrow keys, press Num Lock again, and the NUM indicator will disappear from the status line.

# Navigating in the Worksheet

Think of your screen as a window to the worksheet. Just as you get a different perspective of the outside world depending on which window of your home you look through, you can change your view of the worksheet by looking at different parts of it. You can move from one cell to another, or speed to a distant location using special keys.

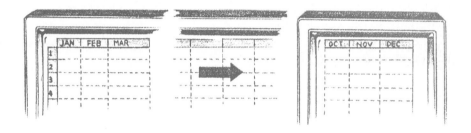

## Basic ARROW Key Options

Although they move only one cell at a time, the ARROW keys take you in any direction. From cell A1, the UP ARROW and LEFT ARROW only cause 1-2-3 to beep, since you cannot move any farther from that cell in those two directions. Depending on your keyboard type, you will find the ARROW keys on the numeric keypad or on separate keys to the left of the keypad.

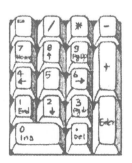

*Tip: Remember that if you use the ARROW keys on the keypad, you will need to ensure that NUM LOCK is not enabled. NUM appears in the status line if NUM LOCK is on. You will need to press NUM LOCK again to turn it off.*

## Keyboard Differences

There is no "standard" keyboard that is used with all computers. The configuration of your keyboard depends on the make and model of the computer you are using. 1-2-3 can be used with most commonly used keyboards. If you need to work with a keyboard that is different from the one you normally use, take a few minutes to find the special keys that 1-2-3 needs, such as HOME, ESC, /, \, NUM LOCK, ENTER, BACKSPACE, the ARROW keys, and the function keys, labeled **F1** through **F10** or **F12**.

As you move around the worksheet, you will relocate the *cell pointer* (the highlighted bar); this pointer indicates the cell that is currently *active*. To determine the address of the active cell, look at the highlighted column letter above the cell pointer, and the highlighted row number to the left of it in the worksheet border. You can also look in the top line of the control panel for this same information.

## Changing the Area Displayed

Starting from cell A1, if you move the cell pointer far enough down or to the right edge of the worksheet, you will come to the end of the *display area*. Moving one more cell down or to the right causes the visible area of the worksheet to change. One column at the left or one row at the top will *scroll* out of the display area, and a new row or column will take its place. As you continue to move in that direction, additional rows or columns will scroll out of the display area at the top or left as new rows and columns come into view. A1 will no longer be the cell displayed in the upper-left corner of the display. If you move the pointer back in the opposite direction until you reach the top or left edge of the worksheet, these rows or columns will scroll back into view as rows or columns from the bottom or right side of the screen disappear.

Don't worry—any data you have in the cells that disappear from view as you move around the display area are not lost; all you're changing is the part of the worksheet you are looking at. You may want to practice moving the cell pointer beyond the edges of the worksheet until you are comfortable with how it works.

## Some Quick Moves

One way to reach
any location on
the worksheet
is to hold

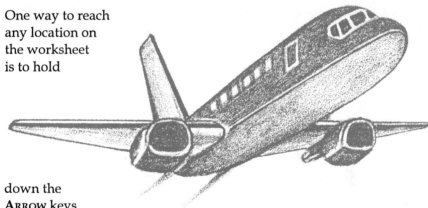

down the
**Arrow** keys
or press them

numerous times—but this will take some time if you need to move from A1 to IV8192. Luckily, 1-2-3 gives you numerous *shortcut keys* to speed your journey. Using these special keys is like hopping a jet flight from New York to Washington: you get there in a very short time.

To move up or down one screen at a time, you can use the **Page Up** and **Page Down** keys. The cell pointer stays positioned at the top of the screen, but an entire screen of new rows will be displayed. The column locations will not change at all. So if the cell pointer is in A1, with A1 through H20 displayed on the screen, pressing **PAGE DOWN** makes A21 through H40 appear, and the cell pointer will be in A21.

To move from side to side one screen at a time, you can press **CTRL-RIGHT ARROW** or **CTRL-LEFT ARROW**. For example, with A1 through H20 displayed, pressing **CTRL-RIGHT ARROW** changes the displayed cells to I1 through P20. Even if a worksheet containing data has had its column widths changed so that a different number of columns is displayed in a single screen, the shift in the display with **CTRL-RIGHT ARROW** or **CTRL-LEFT ARROW** is always one screen of information.

## Two Special Keys: HOME and GoTo

You can quickly return to the A1 location from anywhere on the worksheet. All you need to do is press the **HOME** key from READY mode. Instantly, the cell pointer is repositioned at A1 and the worksheet shifts so that A1 is in the upper-left corner of the display area.

The **GoTo** key takes you from any location to any location, instantly. You will not find a key on your keyboard labeled GoTo, however. GoTo is the name given to the function key, **F5**, when you are using 1-2-3. Function keys may perform different tasks with each software package that you use. So, although **F5** is always the GoTo key in 1-2-3, when you use other software the same **F5** key may print or save your data.

To use **F5** (GoTo) to relocate your cell pointer, press the key one time. It displays this message in the control panel:

```
Enter address to go to:
```

Type the cell address that you want to go to, and your typed entry appears in the control panel next to the prompt. Next, press **ENTER**. Immediately, 1-2-3 adjusts the display, if necessary, and relocates the cell pointer.

# Using 1-2-3's Help

If you had a 1-2-3 expert at the desk next to yours, you could ask for help with 1-2-3 whenever you needed it. Although Lotus does not provide an expert with your package, 1-2-3 does include a *help system* that will answer many of your basic questions. You can always consult 1-2-3's help whenever you are uncertain of the next step.

To activate the 1-2-3 help system, press **F1** (HELP). The help display you receive depends on what you are doing when you request help. You can point to one of the highlighted topics on the help display, or in the help index, and press ENTER to see another help screen for the topic you selected. When you are finished with the help system and want to return to the current task, press Esc. Everything in the worksheet will be just as you left it.

# Keys to Success

Getting comfortable with the 1-2-3 worksheet and your location on it are important first steps in using 1-2-3. From the beginning you will want to make use of the information that 1-2-3 gives you in the control panel at the top of the screen and the status line at the bottom. This information ensures that you are in sync with what 1-2-3 is doing and prevents the feeling of frustration that many new users experience.

There are many different keys that you can use to change the location of the cell pointer on the worksheet. Although you may not want to memorize all of them as you begin, the most important ones to remember are the ARROW keys, the HOME key, and the **F5** (GoTo) key.

And remember—when you need assistance with 1-2-3's features, press **F1** (HELP). A screen of help information is displayed immediately, and many other help topics are only a keystroke or two away. Pressing Esc puts you right back in the worksheet where you left off.

# *What Do They Mean By . . . ?*

**Cell**    A unique location on the worksheet formed by the intersection of a row and column.

**Cell Address**    The column letter plus the row number of the column/ row intersection that is a location where you can store data.

**Cell Pointer**    The highlighted bar that marks your location on the worksheet.

**Control Panel**    The top three lines of the worksheet screen that provide information on the current cell and task.

**Status Line**    The bottom line of the screen that displays error messages and other 1-2-3 indicators.

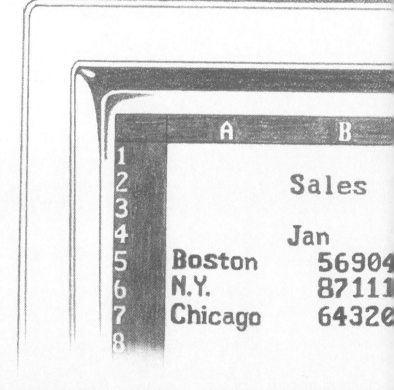

# Making and Saving Worksheet Entries

| C | D | E |
|---|---|---|

Projections

| eb | Mar |
|---|---|
| 64500 | 72900 |
| 93100 | 99750 |
| 75400 | 81995 |

To create a manual ledger, entries are made on lines within the columns of a sheet of ledger paper. To create a worksheet with 1-2-3, the procedure is similar—entries are made in various rows within the columns of the worksheet on screen. The entire worksheet with its entries is known as a *model*.

When you fill out a manual ledger, your entries are either numbers that can be used in computations, or descriptive text. Likewise, with 1-2-3 your entries are either *values*, that can be used in computations, or *labels*, that are used to describe the data stored on the worksheet. Unlike a manual ledger, however, the value entries in 1-2-3 can also be *formulas* that are recomputed any time an adjustment is made to one of the values that the formula references.

### ABC COMPANY
### BALANCE SHEET

| Assets | Division - A | Division - B |
|--------|--------------|--------------|
| Cash | 6 0 0 0 0 0 | 7 0 0 0 0 0 |
| Accounts Rec. | 1 2 0 0 0 0 | 5 0 0 0 0 |
| | | |
| | | |
| | | |

# Making Entries on the Worksheet

Cell entries are like the bricks that are used to build a house. They are added one by one until the model is complete. 1-2-3 supports two different types of cell entries: *labels* and *values*. Every model—from the simplest totaling of expenses to a complex sales projection—consists of nothing more than label and value entries.

## Entering Labels

Labels form the framework of your model. When used at the left end of rows and the top of columns, labels define the contents of the rows and

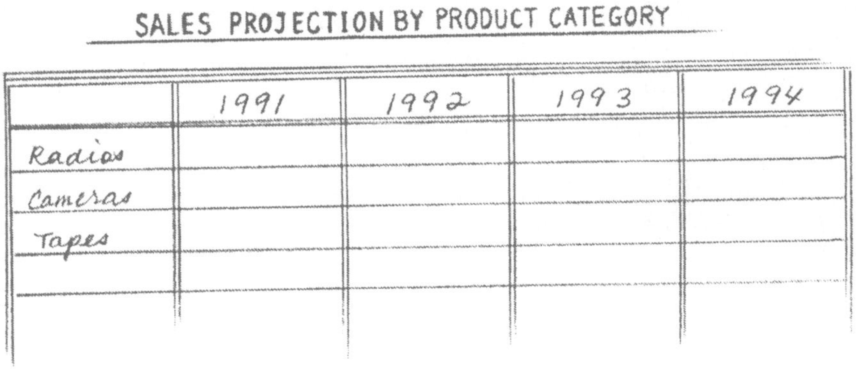

SALES PROJECTION BY PRODUCT CATEGORY

| | 1991 | 1992 | 1993 | 1994 |
|---|---|---|---|---|
| Radios | | | | |
| Cameras | | | | |
| Tapes | | | | |

columns, providing a description of the numbers that you enter or compute. Labels are also used when you need alphabetic characters within the columns, to list part numbers, street addresses, or employee names. Any character that you can type—alphabetic, numeric, or punctuation—can be entered as a label.

## Label Indicators

1-2-3 supports three *label indicators* that change the alignment of text within a cell. These label indicators and their effect on label alignment are as follows:

' Left-aligns the label

*(continued)*

" Right-aligns the label

^ Centers the label

If your cell entry begins with a number, or character that 1-2-3 considers a value character, the entry will be treated as a value—unless you add a label indicator yourself. For example, when you type entries such as addresses or telephone numbers, you will need to begin your entry with a label indicator, or 1-2-3 will not accept your entry. The problem is that 1-2-3 does not recognize the alphabetic street name after the street number as acceptable characters in a value entry.

In all releases of 1-2-3 except 3.0 and 3.1, label entries are limited to 240 characters. These later two releases support entries of as many as 512 characters.

To place a label in a cell, just begin typing, using any first character except 0-9, . + – or (.

*Note: If you must use one of these value characters as the first character in a label, type a specific label indicator first (see "Label Indicators" just above). Then, whatever your entry, that first character that you typed changes the mode indicator from READY to LABEL until the entry is finalized.*

Before *finalizing* your entry, you can always correct any errors by pressing the BACKSPACE key to delete and retype previous characters. (You'll learn more about correcting errors later in this chapter.) To finalize your entry, you can press either ENTER or an ARROW key. When you finalize the entry, it is displayed in the worksheet cell.

The entries in the worksheet illustrated next are made by typing the characters in each cell and pressing the DOWN ARROW after each entry.

Enter this data in a blank worksheet on your own computer, using the same cells that are shown in the following illustration. Remember to press the **Down Arrow** after you type each entry.

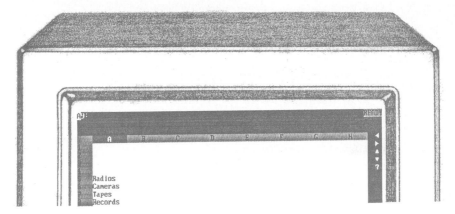

Since the *default width* for a cell is only nine characters, labels longer than that will not fit within a cell. When the cell to the right is empty, the longer labels will borrow display space from these other cells; the entire entry is stored, however, in the cell where it was originally entered. When you need to edit a long label, you will edit the cell where you initially made the entry. In this next illustration, the long label in B3 is borrowing space from C3, D3, and E3. Enter this label on your own screen, starting in cell B3.

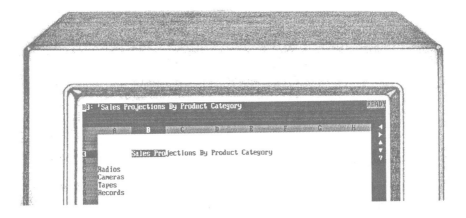

*Tip: Remember—As long as you begin with a label indicator, you can also type numbers as labels. Do this whenever you want to control the alignment of a number and do not want to use the number in a calculation.*

1. In a blank worksheet, move the cell pointer to B4.

2. Type **"1991** and press the RIGHT ARROW.

3. Type **"1992** and press the RIGHT ARROW.

4. Type **"1993** and press the RIGHT ARROW.

5. Type **"1994** and press ENTER.

Your worksheet now looks like this:

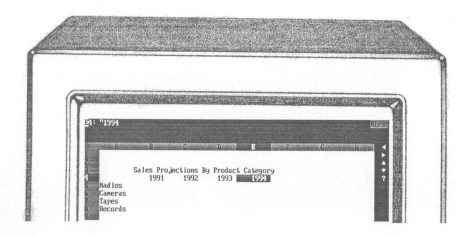

## Entering Values

*Values* can be either numbers or formulas that make a computation. You can enter either whole numbers or numbers with decimal fractions. For a value entry, you can use the numbers 0 through 9, the . + - $ ( ) symbols, and the E @ ^ % symbols, as long as they don't begin the entry.

1-2-3 can accommodate numbers much larger or smaller than the default nine-character cell width. Unlike long labels, however, space is never borrowed to display long numbers. Using the default format for numbers, a number that is too large for its cell is displayed in *scientific notation*. This format indicates the power of 10 by which the displayed number must be multiplied. If you enter a number like 375789155, for example, the displayed entry in scientific notation looks like this:

*0.000194*

*389715*     3

*41794*     9.99999

*32*

*0.05*

---

3.7E+08

---

When a number is extremely small, it will also be displayed in scientific notation.

At the beginning of numbers less than 1, 1-2-3 adds a zero, so .33, for example, appears as 0.33. When a number has more digits *after* the decimal point than 1-2-3 can fit in the column, the number is rounded. As you widen the column, additional decimal places in the number will display.

Remember—1-2-3 determines what is being entered in a cell by the first character you type. If you want an entry to be a label rather than a value, you can add a label indicator as the first character, or start the entry with an alphabetic character.

Add some values to your worksheet.

1. With the cell pointer in E4, press the DOWN ARROW once and the LEFT ARROW three times to move to B5.

2. Type **500** and press the **Down Arrow**. Then type **200** and press the **Down Arrow**. Then type **1200** and press the **Down Arrow**. Finally, type **1900** and press **Enter**.

3. Press the **Up Arrow** three times and the **Right Arrow** once to move to C5.

4. Type **750** and press the **Down Arrow**. Then type **350** and press the **Down Arrow**. Then type **1500** and press the **Down Arrow**. Type **1850** and press **Enter**.

5. Press the **Up Arrow** three times and the **Right Arrow** once to move to D5.

6. Type **900** and press the **Down Arrow**. Then type **450** and press the **Down Arrow**. Then type **5000** and press the **Down Arrow**. Type **1800** and press **Enter**.

7. Press the **Up Arrow** three times and the **Right Arrow** once to move to E5.

8. Type **1050** and press the **Down Arrow**. Then type **800** and press the **Down Arrow**. Then type **7500** and press the **Down Arrow**. Type **1750** and press **Enter**.

Your worksheet now looks like this:

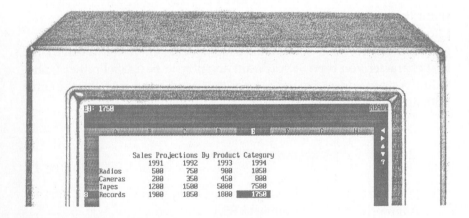

# Correcting Entries in the Worksheet

You have already read that you can use the BACKSPACE key to correct cell entries as you type them. But what if you have already finalized an entry?

1-2-3 gives you several methods for changing incorrect worksheet entries that you have already finalized. The choice depends on the length of the entry and the extent of the change. The decision you make is similar to one you might make for major or minor corrections to a letter produced on a typewriter. If the change is small, you might use white-out fluid; for a more extensive revision, you would probably start fresh with a new sheet of paper. 1-2-3 provides the choice of retyping or editing the entry.

## Retyping the Entry

To replace a number or a short label with another entry, the simplest approach is to retype the entry. When you type the new entry, it displays in the *edit* or *input line*, which is the third line in the control panel. Press ENTER to finalize your new entry, and it appears in the cell, erasing the old entry.

## Using the 1-2-3 Edit Feature

When you notice a mistake in a long entry, you won't want to retype the whole thing. A better method is to *edit* the entry, making the necessary corrections. To edit an entry, you need to place 1-2-3 in EDIT mode. Do this by pressing **F2** (EDIT) from READY, LABEL, or VALUE mode. This means that you can change an entry that is already finalized or alter one that has not yet been finalized.

Once you're in EDIT mode, notice that the cell entry appears on the edit line. You can use the LEFT and RIGHT ARROW keys to move within the entry. Characters that are not needed can be deleted with BACKSPACE if they precede the cursor, or with the DEL key if they are positioned above the cursor. In EDIT mode, you can move to the beginning of an entry by pressing the HOME key and to the end of the entry by pressing the END key.

# Erasing Entries from the Worksheet

Cell entries that are no longer needed can be removed from the worksheet. Many new users attempt to erase an unneeded entry by replacing it with a space, but this is not a good approach. A cell with a space is not an empty cell, since it contains a label consisting of a single space.

To eliminate one or more cell entries on the worksheet, use the /Range Erase command. Think of this command as your eraser to eliminate a group of entries. If you want to eliminate the entire worksheet of entries, you will want to use /Worksheet Erase and confirm the erasure with Yes. Think of this command as a request for a new sheet of electronic paper on which you can start fresh. You will learn how to use these commands in the sections that follow.

## Erasing a Range of Cells

You can eliminate the entry from one cell or from a group of adjacent cells. To erase a range, you will need to invoke a 1-2-3 *command*. 1-2-3 commands are invoked by typing a slash to activate the main menu, and then typing the highlighted letter of the desired command.

## About Ranges

Any rectangular group of adjacent cells is a *range*. A *range address* looks like this: A1..D6, where A1 is the first cell in the range and D6 is the last cell in the range.

*(continued)*

Using a range lets you perform the same action on all the adjacent cells of the range. Commands that work on a range of cells at one time are like pieces of automatic machinery that apply a task to several items at a time. For example, if you are running a farm, you can plant each seedling separately, or you can use machinery to plant many seedlings at once. In 1-2-3, you can use a single command with a range address to repeat an action several times, such as erasing the contents of a group of cells.

To try this now, move the cell selector to the first cell you want to erase, and then type /RE to select the /Range Erase command. You'll be prompted for the range to erase, and 1-2-3 suggests the current cell as a range address, as in A1..A1. (Even a single cell is a range.)

You want to erase a larger range (the current cell and some others, too), so press the RIGHT or DOWN ARROW key enough times to designate the range you want to erase. Notice that it is highlighted on the screen and that the control panel reflects the range address that corresponds to the highlighted cells. Press ENTER, and the range is erased.

If you enter the /Range Erase command first, before positioning the cell selector, you'll need to press Esc to change the suggested range address in the control panel to a single-cell address. Then press the ARROW keys to move the cell pointer to the first cell you wish to erase. Press ENTER to erase this single cell, or type a period and then use the ARROW keys to designate the rest of the range. When you are ready, press ENTER to execute the /Range Erase command.

## /Range Erase

The /Range Erase command allows you to erase the entry in one or more cells. You can specify a range as small as one cell or as large as all the entries in the worksheet.

## Erasing the Entire Worksheet

Erasing the entire worksheet is like tearing the top sheet from a tablet of paper to start fresh on a new sheet. If you want to eliminate every entry on the worksheet, type the / that invokes the main menu, and then select Worksheet Erase Yes. A new worksheet appears on the screen. The old worksheet is gone—unless you saved it to disk before erasing. You'll learn how to do this next.

## /Worksheet Erase

This command erases the entire worksheet without saving the entries first. To prevent accidental loss of data, 1-2-3 asks you to confirm this command by selecting Yes.

# *Saving a File*

The entries you make on a 1-2-3 worksheet are not saved automatically. If the power to your system is turned off, or if something else happens to take you out of 1-2-3, all of your work will be lost.

You need to keep a permanent copy of your completed work—either on a floppy disk or on your hard disk—just as you keep a file of important papers for later use at home or in the office. Think of saving a file as placing your information in an envelope and writing a name on it to identify it. In 1-2-3, you can use TAXES90, for example, as a *filename*, just as you might label an envelope so you'll know it contains your 1990 tax records.

## About Filenames

To distinguish one file from another, you need to provide a unique name for each file on the disk. In assigning this name, you must follow the rules of the DOS operating system; DOS limits you to a filename of no more than eight characters. When you create files of your 1-2-3 worksheets, 1-2-3 automatically adds a *filename extension* to each filename you create, so the longest filename you will see totals eleven characters. .WK1 is the filename extension for Release 2.01, 2.2, and 2.3. Release 3 and 3.1 use .WK3 as the extension. When you save a file with Release 1A, .WKS is added as the extension. So if you have a file in Release 2.3 with the name BUDGET, the actual filename is BUDGET.WK1.

## Valid Filenames

1-2-3 follows the rules for filenames established by the DOS operating system. You can assign any name using from one to eight characters. You cannot use spaces and some symbols in filenames. You should restrict your selection to characters from A-Z, 0-9, and the underscore (_). Using these guidelines means your filenames will be compatible with all releases of DOS.

Here's how to save and name a file:

1.  Invoke the 1-2-3 menu by typing a /.

2. Type **F** to select File, and then type **S** to choose Save. 1-2-3 prompts you for a filename with this message:

```
Enter name of file to save:
```

3. In response to this prompt, type a filename and press ENTER.

A permanent copy of the file is saved to the default disk drive and directory.

Saving a file that is already on the disk (perhaps you have added something to it or changed it) requires an extra step. Once you type **/FS** to invoke File Save, you do not need to type the filename because it is already displayed in the control panel. You need only to press ENTER. Now comes the extra step: type an **R**, to select Replace, in response to the next prompt. 1-2-3 replaces the copy of the file on the disk with the edited file currently stored in memory.

## /File Save

The **/File Save** command saves a copy of the worksheet as it is stored in memory to a floppy disk or the hard disk. After you type a filename and press ENTER, the def⸱⸱ drive and directory will be used automatically to stored on the disk, you will need to confirm

If the file is alread⸱ its replacement

# *Retrieving a File*

To read a file from disk and place it into memory so you can work with it, use the /File Retrieve command. This is just like finding the envelope that contains the information you want and opening it. /File Retrieve auto-matically erases any worksheet that is currently in memory before reading in the new file. So remember to save the file you're working on before you retrieve a new one.

## /File Retrieve

The /File Retrieve command reads the default drive and directory on the disk and displays a list of the worksheet files that it finds. When you highlight a filename and press ENTER, the file is displayed as the current worksheet.

Retrieving a file is simple. First type / to invoke the main menu. Next, type an F to select File and an R to select Retrieve. In the control panel, 1-2-3 displays the names of the first couple of files in the current directory, as shown here:

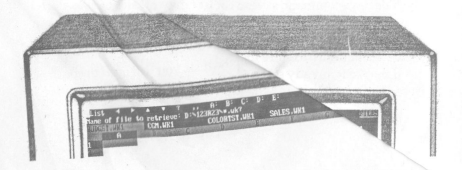

To retrieve the file you want, you can type the name of the file and press ENTER. Another, quicker approach may be to press the RIGHT ARROW until the file that you want to use is highlighted (the list scrolls within the control panel as you continue to press RIGHT ARROW), and then press ENTER.

## Keys to Success

You can enter both labels and values on the worksheet. Labels are descriptive text; they include information such as the months of the year or account names. Values are numbers, or formulas that define a calculation. Either type of entry can be placed in any worksheet cell.

You can retype entries to replace them. You can also use the F2 (EDIT) key to make a change to an entry without retyping it. If you need to erase entries altogether, you can use /Range Erase to eliminate a single cell or a range of cells. To erase the entire worksheet you can use /Worksheet Erase Yes.

To save a file, you use /File Save and type a filename consisting of from one to eight characters. When you press ENTER, 1-2-3 adds a filename extension and saves the file to disk. Spaces and special characters other than the underscore (_) should not be used in a filename.

To retrieve a file from your disk, you use /File Retrieve.

## What Do They Mean By . . . ?

Cursor    The small flashing line that marks your place in an entry in VALUE, LABEL, or EDIT mode.

Default    The initial setting for a specific 1-2-3 feature.

Edit    To change an entry without retyping the entire entry.

**Edit Line**     The third line of the control panel at the top of the screen.

**Label**     An entry that contains text.

**Label Prefix**     A one-character indicator that determines the alignment of a label in a cell and tells 1-2-3 to accept numbers in that label.

**Range**     A group of cells, with a cell address such as A1..D6, treated as a unit for a 1-2-3 command.

**Scientific Notation**     A concise format for recording very large or very small numbers that displays the number as a power of ten, such as 4.09 E+08 or –.8 E – 06.

**Value**     An entry containing only numbers and symbols needed to record numeric entries and arithmetic operations.

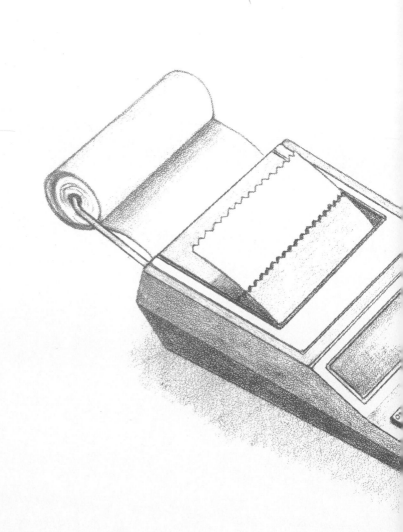

# Performing Calculations

1-2-3 is ideal for handling all your calculations. Whether you are calculating your net pay or mortgage payment, the proceeds of the office coffee fund, your business's sales projections, or the cost of maintenance on your office complex, 1-2-3 can provide a quick solution.

Before buying 1-2-3, you probably did your computations on a scrap of paper or a calculator. The paper-and-pencil method usually works about as well as whatever mood you're in that day. Step up to a calculator, and you gain the advantage of being able to perform computations without an error—no matter how many calculations you ask it to perform in a day.

1-2-3 offers the same error-free performance as a sophisticated calculator—with even more advantages. For example, when you use a calculator you have to reenter the whole sequence of arithmetic steps each time you have new data. With 1-2-3, you simply define your calculations once; to get a new result, you only need to enter new data for the calculation to act on.

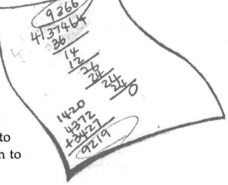

# *What Is a Formula?*

A *formula* defines a computation you want 1-2-3 to perform. To 1-2-3, a formula entry in a cell is a value entry, just like the numbers you entered in the previous chapter. When you enter a formula you are telling 1-2-3 the precise steps it needs to obtain an answer. A formula is like a recipe—except it refers to cells and the values stored in them rather than food ingredients.

Many new users are intimidated by formula entry. Don't be daunted by this task, however—it is no more difficult than explaining to your assistant which numbers need to be added or multiplied to get an answer.

If you can tell someone to multiply the number of hours worked by the hourly pay rate, you'll be able to define the same steps to 1-2-3, too.

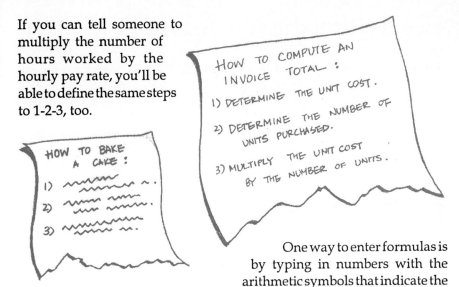

One way to enter formulas is by typing in numbers with the arithmetic symbols that indicate the operations you want to perform. For instance, you could type **4+5** in a cell; this tells 1-2-3 to add the numbers 4 and 5 together.

A better approach, though, is to store the numbers you want to use for calculations in various worksheet cells, and then build the formula using references to those cells rather than the numbers themselves. Suppose the numbers to be added are stored in A2 and B4; the formula to add these numbers would be written as +A2+B4. (The extra + is needed in front of the *A* at the beginning of the formula to tell 1-2-3 not to treat the entry as a label.) Only the result of the calculation is displayed in the worksheet cell; the formula itself appears in the control panel when your cell pointer is on the cell.

1-2-3 provides some helpful prerecorded formulas called *@functions*. The @functions save you time because their computation is already defined—all you need to do is to give the @function the data it needs to work. It's like having an electric slide rule at your disposal. We'll explore @functions more thoroughly later in this chapter.

# *The Arithmetic Operators*

Arithmetic *operators* are road signs that guide 1-2-3 through your formulas, ensuring that you get the correct results. The most important arithmetic operations are multiplication, division, addition, and subtraction.

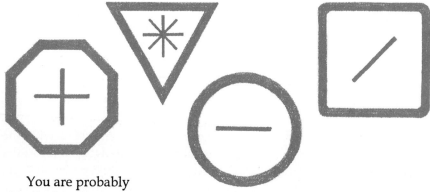

You are probably already familiar with the operators for addition and subtraction (+ and –) because you use these same symbols when you record calculations on paper.

The multiplication and division operations are often represented in paper calculations with x and ÷, respectively, but you will need to use different symbols with 1-2-3. 1-2-3 uses the * as the multiplication operator. Thus, entering +A4*F5 in a cell tells 1-2-3 to take the current contents of A4 and multiply them by the contents of F5. For division, 1-2-3 uses the / operator. So +A4/G5 tells 1-2-3 to divide the number stored in A4 by the number in G5.

## Priority of Operations

When you use a calculator, operations are performed in the order you enter them. With 1-2-3, operations are not always computed in entry order. Instead, 1-2-3 waits for you to finalize the entire formula, and then analyzes its contents. The mathematical operations in your formula are performed in a specific order, called the *priority of operations*. It works like this: First 1-2-3 scans for parentheses and evaluates the operations within them, starting with the innermost set of parentheses. 1-2-3 next scans again from left to right, looking for multiplication and division operators, and performs those operations. Then 1-2-3 scans for addition and subtraction operators, and performs those operations.

If you have difficulty remembering the priority order, visualize your dear Aunt Sally with a cookie jar, and think of asking, "Please, My Dear Aunt Sally." The first

**Please My Dear Aunt Sally**

letters of the words in this mnemonic phrase will remind you of the order that 1-2-3 uses when evaluating formulas.

# Overriding the Default Priority

Getting your formulas to come out with the right answers often requires the addition of a pair of parentheses to your formulas. Remember—1-2-3 evaluates the numbers in the parentheses first; outside the parentheses, the default priority order is used.

Suppose you want to compute the cost of ordering seven chairs that each cost $100, plus $4.50 in shipping charges. If you enter 100+4.50*7, you will get an answer of $131.50, rather than the correct result of $731.00. To obtain the correct answer from 1-2-3, you need to use parentheses around the addition operation so that it is evaluated first. The formula (100+4.5)*7 will provide the result you want, which is adding 100 to 4.5 and then multiplying that result by 7.

# The @Functions: 1-2-3's Free Formulas

All of 1-2-3's built-in @functions can be used by simply typing them into a cell. 1-2-3 has up to 103 @functions (depending on the 1-2-3 release you are using), ranging from statistical and financial calculations to trigonometric functions.

Using @functions means that you don't need to enter lengthy formulas. The formulas you need are built right into the @function, so you just need to tell 1-2-3 what data to use. This data you provide is known as an *argument*. Think of an argument as a piece of information needed to get the

$90,000.00
10% INTEREST
20 YEARS
$ 868.52/MONTH

correct result. For example, if you want 1-2-3 to compute a loan payment, you need to specify the loan balance, the interest rate, and for how long you want to borrow the money. These three arguments are what 1-2-3 has to know to understand what type of loan the payment is for.

To use any of 1-2-3's @functions in a cell, type @, the function name, an opening parenthesis, any arguments, and a closing parenthesis. For example, the entry @SUM(A1..A100) tells 1-2-3 to add all the values stored in the range A1..A100. When you enter @functions, keep these guidelines in mind:

- Do not enter spaces in the @function formula, just as you do not enter spaces in other formulas you enter.

- When an @function uses several arguments, separate the arguments with commas—as in @SUM(A1,B10,C20) to add the values in A1, B10, and C20.

- Some @functions can be used in only one way and do not use arguments or parentheses. For example, when you want to represent the value of *pi*, which is 3.14159, you only need to enter @ $\pi$.

The arguments that an @function uses depend on the information the function needs. For example, @SUM needs to know which values to add, so its arguments are the values, cells, and ranges that it should add. A function like @PMT, which calculates a loan payment, needs to know the amount you are borrowing, the interest rate, and the term of the loan. These three arguments must be provided in a specific order so that 1-2-3 knows which is which.

To see a list of the available @functions, select @Function List from the Help Index in 1-2-3's help screen. Select the @function you want to know about from the list, and 1-2-3 will display information about that function, including the arguments it needs, and in what order.

# The Building Blocks that Create Your Model

Although formulas produce the important results in your worksheets, the labels and numbers discussed in the previous chapter are just as crucial. You can complete your entries in any order, but typically labels are placed on the worksheet first to establish its structure. Numbers are usually entered next because they are known *constants* and are needed for the formulas to provide results. The third step is adding the formulas.

Putting all the pieces together is frequently called *building a model*. In the next few sections you'll make all the entries necessary to build a model that computes the cost of several purchases.

## Use Labels to Add Meaning to Your Formula Results

Entering labels establishes a structure for the rest of your entries. Let's begin to construct the model to record the cost of purchasing several supply items. The worksheet label entries look like this:

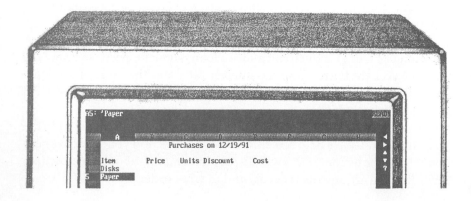

To complete these entries on a blank worksheet on your screen, first type **Purchases on 12/19/91** in C1. Type **Item** in A3, **Price** in B3, **Units** in C3, **Discount** in D3, and **Cost** in E3. Then type **Disks** in A4, and type **Paper** in A5.

# Use Numbers to Provide the Raw Material for the Formulas

Known quantities are recorded as numeric constants in your models. In our example, both price and quantity (units) are known constants for disks and paper, as shown in this next illustration:

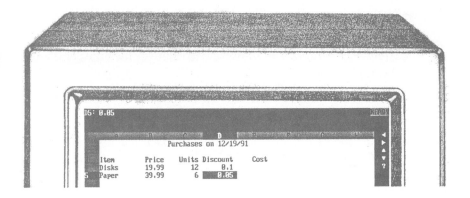

You'll need to enter the following numbers in cells B4 through D5 of your worksheet:

B4:    Enter **19.99**
B5:    Enter **35.99**
C4:    Enter **12**
C5:    Enter **6**
D4:    Enter **.1**
D5:    Enter **.05**

# Add the Formulas to Complete Your Model

The next step needed to build this model is to create two formulas that calculate the cost for each item and total the cost for all items purchased.

1. To enter the first formula, move to E4 and type **+** to tell 1-2-3 that you are entering a formula.

2. Type **B4** to use the value stored in B4, and **∗C4** to multiply the B4 value by the value in C4. *Remember:* Don't type any spaces within a formula.

3. To include the discount, type **−B4∗C4∗D4**. You don't need any parentheses because you want 1-2-3 to multiply the numbers before subtracting any.

4. You have now entered the entire formula, +B4∗C4−B4∗C4∗D4, so press ENTER.

5. To enter the second formula, press the DOWN ARROW, and type **+(B5∗C5)−(B5∗C5∗D5)** in cell E5, and press ENTER. This time you added the parentheses only to group the calculations and improve the readability of the formula. The addition of the parentheses does not alter the order in which 1-2-3 performs the calculation.

Now all that is required is to enter the formula that adds the two costs.

## Adding a Total with @SUM

When you need to add two numbers, you can type a formula like +E4+E5. If you need to add 100 numbers, this type of a formula takes time to enter and is error prone. The most efficient way to add a list of values is to use the @SUM function. For example, consider this @SUM function:

@SUM(50,A1,B5..B105)

This adds 50, the value in A1, and the values in B5 through B105. Notice that all of the values, cells, and ranges are separated by commas.

To use a @SUM function for the invoice, press the DOWN ARROW, type **@SUM(E4..E5)** in cell E6, and press ENTER. This formula adds the results of the other two formulas. In this instance, using @SUM instead of a + operator to add the values is not a significant timesaver, but in a situation when you have many numbers to add, @SUM's usefulness will be more apparent.

Your final model looks like this:

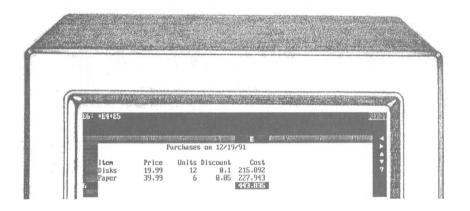

You could have used paper and pencil to calculate the values in this worksheet, but instead you've let 1-2-3 do what it does best: repeat the same calculation and keep the results up-to-date. If you had done this on paper, the next time you want to order disks and paper you would have to perform all of the calculations again. With 1-2-3, you can enter any new information—for the item, price, quantity, or discount—and 1-2-3 will calculate the new purchase price for you.

Suppose you change the model so the invoice will calculate how much it would cost to order two disk drives and three monitors. Since 1-2-3 is so flexible, you can adjust your worksheet for more applications. To try this, move to B4, type **15.99**, and press ENTER. Move to C5, type **15**, and press ENTER. Notice how 1-2-3 updates the values in E4, E5, and E6 as you make new entries. This is called *recalculation*.

Your new and up-to-date worksheet looks like this:

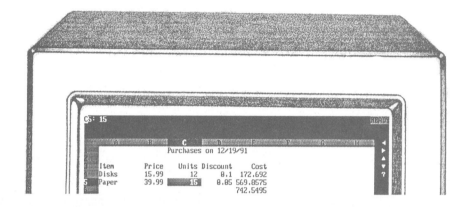

With your model now built, you are ready to save it by typing /**FS** for the /**F**ile **S**ave command. Type **INVOICE** for the filename and press **ENTER**.

## *Keys to Success*

Formulas are the backbone of worksheet models. Although they take more time to record and test than other worksheet entries, formulas are what really save you time in a worksheet. Once you have defined your computations, the model is available forever.

You can record formulas with numeric constants or cell references. Cell references are best because 1-2-3 updates the formula result immediately whenever the value in a referenced cell is changed.

Special symbols called arithmetic operators are used to indicate computations you want 1-2-3 to perform. The * represents multiplication, / represents division, + represents addition, and – represents subtraction. In evaluating a formula, 1-2-3 performs multiplication and division first, before addition and subtraction. To change the priority order, you can enclose operations within parentheses; 1-2-3 performs these operations first.

# What Do They Mean By . . . ?

**Argument**    A piece of information an @function needs to calculate the correct result.

**Arithmetic Operator**    A special symbol used to represent a computation that you want 1-2-3 to perform, such as *, /, + and –.

**@Function**    A prerecorded formula that the 1-2-3 software provides.

**Formula**    A recorded set of instructions that 1-2-3 will follow in performing a computation.

**Model**    A worksheet representation of a series of computations used to solve a repetitive problem.

**Priority of Operations**    The order in which the various operators used in a formula are evaluated.

**Recalculation**    1-2-3's process of updating the results of computations as values on the worksheet change.

# Printing the Worksheet 5

Printing your worksheets on paper lets you share them with others, include them in reports, and otherwise make practical use of your work. Or you may just want to be able to see a large model all at once, instead of just a small section of it on the screen.

Before you can print in 1-2-3, you must use the Install program (see Appendix A) to select the text printer you will use. If you do not select a printer, 1-2-3 will not print your worksheets properly.

If you have a printer available and selected, you can print either the entire worksheet or just a small section. You can accept 1-2-3's default settings for the print process or you can customize how the printed output will look—either way, you will be pleased with the results if you follow the simple rules outlined in this chapter. Here's a sample of what you'll get with 1-2-3's default settings:

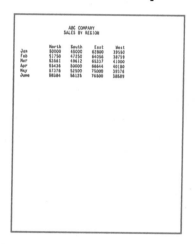

# Controlling the Quality of Printed Output

Printing using 1-2-3's Print menu uses only the basic features of a printer. This means that your printed worksheets, though clear and presentable for most uses, will not display the special fonts and graphics your printer may be able to employ. Each release of 1-2-3 supports its own set, of advanced print features. For

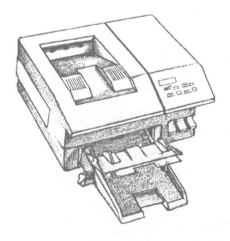

example, in Chapter 12
you will learn about
using Wysiwyg mode to
enhance the print
capabilities of 1-2-3
Releases 2.3 and 3.1.

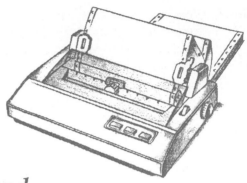

# Using the
# /Print Command

The 1-2-3 Print menu contains the commands you need to print a basic
worksheet. Once data is entered on the current worksheet, a few simple
menu selections let you print the model. It's easy—just select the printer,
select the range to print, designate any needed changes to the default print
option settings (such as margins), and then print the worksheet.

To perform printing tasks, first display the main menu by typing a /.
Next, type **P** to select Print, and then type **P** again to select Printer as the
destination of your printed output. Now 1-2-3 displays the main Print
menu:

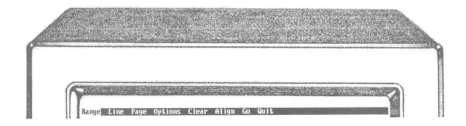

The Print menu contains the major commands you need to print your
worksheet. Regardless of the 1-2-3 release you are using, the Print menu
will contain at least these basic commands. If you are using Release 2.2, 2.3,
or newer versions of 3.1, you will see a display of the current settings for
the Print menu commands. This is called a *settings sheet* (Release 2.2) or
*dialog box* (Release 2.3 and 3.1).

*Note: The Print menu is a "sticky" menu—that is, it remains on the screen until you select Quit by typing Q to tell 1-2-3 that you want to return to READY mode. You'll come across other sticky menus as you use 1-2-3.*

## /Print Printer Quit

This command leaves the Print menu so you can return to READY mode.

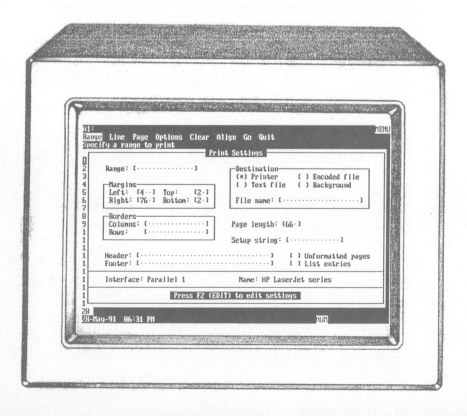

# Defining a Print Range

Once you are in the Print menu, you need to select the worksheet data you want to print. To print any range in the worksheet, choose **Range** on the Print menu and then use your mouse or keyboard to select the range of cells that contains the data you want to print. The range you select is what 1-2-3 prints when you tell it to start.

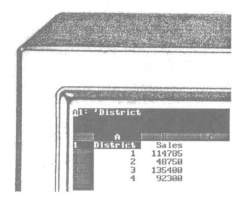

| District | Sales  |
|----------|--------|
| 1        | 114785 |
| 2        | 48750  |
| 3        | 135400 |
| 4        | 92300  |

If your worksheet has long labels that borrow display space from blank cells to the right, don't forget to include these borrowed cells in the range to be printed. For example, suppose you are printing this data:

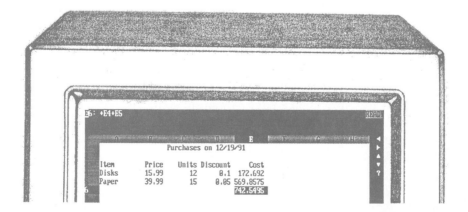

The label in C1 also displays in D1 and E1. When you print this data, you'll need to include columns C through E in the print range, so that 1-2-3 prints the entire label stored in C1.

When you select a range for printing, 1-2-3's /Print command remembers it. You can print the same data again without having to specify its range address again because 1-2-3 retains the last range address you selected. If you want to print data in a range different from the one 1-2-3 suggests, press Esc or Backspace to remove the existing range address, and select a new one.

## /Print Printer Range

This command sets the worksheet range to print. You can specify a range as small as one cell or as large as all the entries in the worksheet.

## Setting Margins and Page Length

The Print menu has some basic options you may need to change for a given printing task.

- Often you will want to change the *margins* to alter the amount of data 1-2-3 prints on a page. A margin is the distance between the printed data and the left, right, top, or bottom edge of the paper. Think of the margins as a frame of white space around your data to make it more readable and attractive.

- 1-2-3 by default prints 66 lines per page. If your printer prints a different number of lines on a page, you will want to change the *page length* setting so that 1-2-3 puts the proper amount of data on each page.

## *Measuring Margins*

1-2-3 does not measure margins in distances, such as inches. Instead, the *left* and *right* margins are measured by the *number of characters* reserved for the margins. For example, a left margin of 10 means the left margin is wide enough to accommodate ten characters. The right margin is defined by the number of characters from the left edge of the page where the right margin begins. 1-2-3 has default left and right margins of four characters on both sides. If you change your margins to be wider than this, you'll get less data on

```
          ABC COMPANY
        SALES BY REGION

        January February   March    April      May
North   $50,000  $51,750  $53,561  $55,436  $57,376
South   $45,000  $47,250  $49,613  $50,000  $52,500
East    $62,800  $64,056  $65,337  $66,644  $75,000
West    $39,550  $38,759  $41,000  $40,180  $39,376
```

```
          ABC COMPANY
        SALES BY REGION

January  February   March    April      May      June     July    August
$50,000  $51,750  $53,561  $55,436  $57,376  $59,384  $61,463  $63,614
$45,000  $47,250  $49,613  $50,000  $52,500  $55,125  $57,881  $60,775
$62,800  $64,056  $65,337  $66,644  $75,000  $76,500  $78,030  $79,591
$39,550  $38,759  $41,000  $40,180  $39,376  $38,589  $37,817  $37,061
```

a page but the page will have a more balanced look. Narrow margins let you fit as much data as possible on a page.

Top and *bottom* margins in 1-2-3 are measured in *blank lines*. The default setting is two lines at the top and bottom of the worksheet.

## *Measuring Page Length*

The number of *printed lines* that fits on a 1-2-3 page is the total of the number of lines reserved for the top and bottom margins, plus three lines each for the header and footer, plus the number of lines reserved for your data on each page. (When your printing skills become more advanced, you'll learn to design *headers* and *footers*, which are text that you can specify to appear at the top and bottom of every page of your worksheet.)

*Changing the Margins*

- To change the margins for a printed worksheet, select /Print Printer Options Margins. Select the margin you want to change, type the new margin measurement, and press ENTER.

- To change the page length for a printed worksheet, select /Print Printer Options Pg-Length. Type the number of lines you want on the page, and press ENTER.

*Tip: The default page length is 66, but you may want to change it to 60 if you are using a laser printer that fits only 60 lines on a page.*

After setting your margin and page length options, when you are ready to return to the menu, select /Print Printer Quit.

## /Print Printer Options Margins

This command sets the empty space 1-2-3 leaves on all four sides of the page. After selecting the command, choose Left, Right, Top, or Bottom. Then type the number of characters or lines you want for a margin, and press ENTER. Select Quit to return to the main Print menu.

---

## /Print Printer Options Pg-Length

This command sets the total number of lines 1-2-3 prints on each page. Type the number of lines you want to print, and press ENTER. Select Quit to return to the main Print menu.

---

# *Printing the Worksheet*

Once you select the worksheet range to print and specify the print settings you want, you are ready to print your worksheet. To print the invoice totals worksheet you have been working with in this book, follow the steps below (you can make these selections from the active print menu):

1. On the Print menu, type **A** to select **Align**. This tells 1-2-3 that the printer is at the top of the current page.

2. Type **G** for **Go**; this prints the worksheet range you selected. If you specified a range that includes the whole worksheet, your printout will look like the following illustration. Notice that the printed data does not include the column letters and row numbers.

Purchases on 12/19/91

| Item | Price | Units | Discount | Cost |
|------|-------|-------|----------|------|
| Disks | 15.99 | 12 | 0.1 | 172.692 |
| Paper | 39.99 | 15 | 0.05 | 569.8575 |
| | | | | 742.5495 |

3. Type **P** for **Page** to advance the paper in the printer to a blank sheet.

4. Finally, type **Q** for Quit. This exits the Print menu and returns you to READY mode.

If you select **Go**, **Page**, and **Quit** and nothing happens, make sure your printer is turned on and connected to the computer. When you are printing on a network, you may have to wait a few minutes until the network printer prints your worksheet. If you see a message that a printer is not installed, this means you haven't specified a printer using the Install program (as described in Appendix A).

When you print a worksheet that contains more information than will fit on a single page, 1-2-3 will divide the worksheet range into multiple pages.

## /Print Printer Align

This command resets 1-2-3 to assume that the printer is at the top of a page.

## /Print Printer Page

This command advances the paper in the printer to the next blank sheet. Usually, you select this command when you are finished printing, so you can retrieve your page from the printer.

---

## /Print Printer Go

This command prints the currently selected range and then returns
to the Print menu in READY mode.

---

# Keys to Success

You can use 1-2-3's /Print commands to copy the data on your screen to a
piece of paper. Start the printing process by selecting /Print Printer. From
the main Print menu, select Range and the worksheet range to print.

Selecting Options from the main Print menu lets you access simple
print settings such as margins and page length as well as other more
advanced features. Since /Print Printer Options displays a sticky menu,
you can return to the main Print menu by selecting Quit.

To print the worksheet data, select Align, Go, Page, and Quit. 1-2-3
returns you to the worksheet and prints the data.

# What Do They Mean By . . . ?

Dialog Box    In Releases 2.3 and 3.1, a screen for displaying and changing
command options. In this chapter, you worked with the dialog box that
displays the settings for the /Print Printer command options.

Margins    The white space that surrounds text printed on a page.

Page Length    The number of lines that can print on a page.

**Settings Sheet**     In Release 2.2, screen for a command such as **/Print Printer**; it displays the current settings for a group of command options.

**Sticky Menu**     A menu that remains on screen until you select an option that explicitly exits the sticky menu.

|   | A | B | C |
|---|---|---|---|
| 1 |   | 1989 | 1990 |
| 2 | ABC Company | 350000 | 400000 |
| 3 |   |   |   |
| 4 |   |   |   |
| 5 |   |   |   |
| 6 |   |   |   |
| 7 |   |   |   |
| 8 |   |   |   |
| 9 |   |   |   |

# Changing the Appearance of Entries

**6**

All information can be presented in many different ways. A scribbled note to yourself doesn't need to be read by others and may not require a neat appearance to accomplish its purpose. Information on a ledger of a tax return, on the other hand, needs to be entered neatly in its columns since it's important for the reader to see precise information. A wedding invitation may look best when written with calligraphy. In each case the optimal appearance is determined by the information being recorded, its purpose, its audience.

# 1-2-3's Numeric Format Options

1-2-3 provides several appearance options for the numbers on your worksheet. These options can be used for numeric constants as well as the results of formula calculations. When you change the *numeric format*, or how the numbers display, you change only the *appearance* of the number on the worksheet, not the *value* of the number or formula result. For example, you can use formatting to display .55 as .5, but 1-2-3 will use .55 when that cell's value is used in a calculation.

## The Default Numeric Format: General

The default appearance for all numbers is initially set by 1-2-3. This allows you to create a model and get the right answer before focusing on improving the model's appearance. If you are not happy with the default appearance, you can change it.

The default format is called the General format. General format allows the number of decimal places to vary and adds a zero in front of decimal fractions. To ensure that every numeric entry displays, the General format uses scientific notation to display very large numbers and rounds the display of small decimal fractions to fit the width of the column.

As long as General format is in effect, the following entries will not display exactly as you type them (assuming that the column width has not been altered from its default setting of 9):

| Typed Entry | Displayed Entry |
| --- | --- |
| 18349638443 | 1.8E+10 |
| .86342373 | 0.863423 |
| .5 | 0.5 |

## Other Numeric Format Options

There are other format options that change how a number appears. You can display all numbers in the worksheet with the same number of digits after the decimal point, for example. You can also add formatting characters such as commas, currency symbols, and percent signs.

Other numeric display options are more consistent in their display than the General format. Thus numbers in a format other than General that are too large for the current cell width are displayed as asterisks ********. When you see these, 1-2-3 is telling you that you need to select another display format or change the width of the columns containing those entries.

To set the display of numbers in a range, use the /Range Format command. Some of the most common formats are shown in the box entitled "Numeric Formats." With all of the numeric formats (except General), you need to also select how many digits come after the decimal point. Once 1-2-3 knows the format to apply and the number of digits after the decimal point, you can specify the range to be formatted. Press ENTER, and the numbers in the range instantly display with the new format.

Using your invoice worksheet, you can apply some different formats to the ranges to make it look like the worksheet shown here:

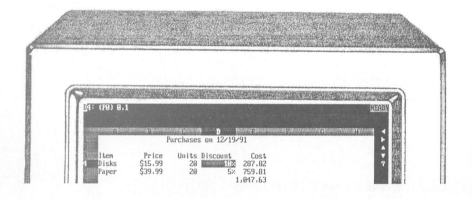

As you work with the numeric format options and the /Range Format command, notice that 1-2-3 displays information in the control panel to describe the formatting that is applied to a cell. This *format indicator* appears in parentheses, in front of the cell's contents. Usually you'll see a character representing the type of format (as in F for Fixed or , for comma), and then the number of digits you've specified to appear after the decimal point.

# Numeric Formats

Here are some of the numeric formats you will want to use in your worksheets:

Fixed
: Displays all numbers with the same number of digits after the decimal point.

Scientific
: Displays numbers using scientific notation.

Currency
: Displays numbers with a $ at the front, a comma separating thousands, and a fixed number of digits after the decimal point.

, (comma)
: Displays numbers with a comma separating thousands and a fixed number of digits after the decimal point.

Percent
: Displays numbers multiplied by 100 with a % at the end.

General
: Displays numbers in 1-2-3's default format.

# /Range Format

This command applies a format to a range of numbers. After selecting the command, choose one of the formats. If appropriate, type the number of digits to display after the decimal point. Then press ENTER. Specify the range to use the format, and press ENTER again.

# Changing the Width of a Column

All columns on a new worksheet are initially nine characters wide. As you've learned already, labels that contain more than nine characters will borrow display space from adjacent empty cells. In contrast, with numbers containing no decimal point, only eight digits will fit in a cell (in General format). This is because 1-2-3 wants to make sure that a number entered in a column has at least one space separating it from the numbers in the adjacent columns.

When a number contains a decimal point, only seven characters will display because the decimal uses one position. Formats that contain special characters, such as a $ or %, use another space for these characters. So remember: Formats other than General allow fewer digits in a given cell.

When you need to, you can make any column either narrower or wider. The default width of nine characters is adequate only when your numbers do not exceed eight characters, since numbers must be one character less than the column width. For most releases of 1-2-3, the maximum column width is 240 and the minimum width is 1.

To set a column's width, first position the cell pointer in the column you want to change. Then select the /Worksheet Column-Width Set-Width command. Once you start the command, you can change the width by either typing a new column width or using the ARROW keys, as explained next.

## Typing a New Column Width

After you type /WCS (Worksheet Column-Width Set-Width), one way to specify the new column width is simply to type the number of characters you want the column to accommodate. For example, to widen a column from 9 to 12, type /WCS and **12**. Then press ENTER, and 1-2-3 instantly displays the column with the new width.

Any cells in the column that displayed asterisks because a nine-character width was too narrow for the values will now display value entries up to 12 characters. Also, long labels may not need to borrow display space from adjoining cells. In the next two illustrations, you can see how widening columns A and B allows the full name of the salesperson to display, along with the complete sales figure in Currency format.

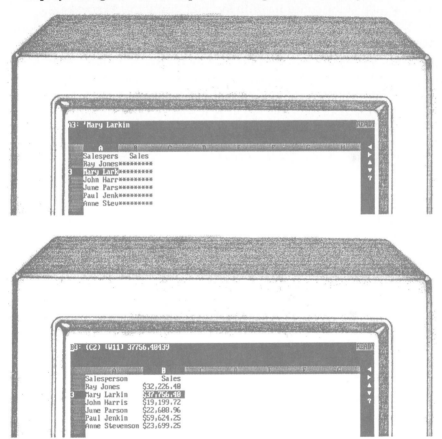

As you work with the /WCS command, notice that when you type in a new column width, 1-2-3 displays your entry in the control panel—this *column-width indicator* is in square brackets [ ], next to the format indicator and before the cell contents, as shown in the preceding illustration.

## Using the ARROW Keys to Set a New Width

Most of the time you won't know exactly how wide you want to make a column. Rather than using the Worksheet Column-Width Set-Width

(/WCS) command several times as you decide on a column width, and having to count the numbers in various entries, there's an easier way—you can adjust the column width by sight, using the ARROW keys.

Once you enter the /WCS command, instead of typing in the column width in response to 1-2-3's prompt, you can press the LEFT ARROW key, and 1-2-3 decreases the column width by 1. Press the RIGHT ARROW, and 1-2-3 increases the column width by 1. Keep pressing either the LEFT or RIGHT ARROW repeatedly until the column looks like it has the width you want, and then press ENTER to finalize it. Just as when you type a number for the column width, the control panel displays the adjusted column-width indicator in square brackets ([ ]).

---

## /Worksheet Column-Width Set-Width

This command changes the width of a column. After entering this command, type the new column width or use the ARROW keys to indicate the new column width and press ENTER to finalize it.

---

# Changing the Alignment of Label Entries

1-2-3 recognizes most of your label entries as you make them, adding the ' label indicator for you at the front of your entry. As you know, this label indicator does not display in the cell with the label but is visible in the control panel. What you do see in the cell is the effect of the label indicator—it causes the label to be left-aligned in the cell.

To achieve a different alignment, just type in a different label indicator. The " indicator causes a label to be right-aligned, and the ^ indicator causes it to be centered.

When you need to alter all the labels in a group of existing cells, you can do it quickly and easily with the /Range Label command. For example, if you enter the months of the year as labels across the columns of a worksheet, and then decide you want them centered or right-aligned, you can use one /Range Label command rather than editing twelve separate cells.

1. Select the /Range Label command (type /RL) from the main menu.

2. Choose Left, Right, or Center for the alignment you want for a range of labels.

3. Specify the range of labels to be realigned (in the following example, B1..M1), and press ENTER.

1-2-3 changes the label indicators of each label in the range to the one you selected; the result is just as if you'd edited each of the cells individually — but by having 1-2-3 do it for you, you've saved time and avoided possible errors.

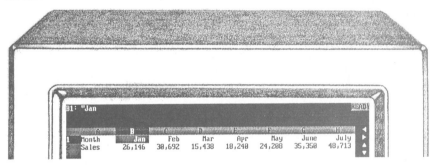

## /Range Label

This command changes the alignment of labels in a range. After entering this command, choose Left, Right, or Center for the alignment, select the range of labels to change, and press ENTER.

# Using Worksheet Windows for a Different Appearance

If you are standing outside a new home wondering about its interior, you might walk around the outside and peer into the various windows. Each window provides a slightly different perspective of the house's interior.

With 1-2-3, you can also create different windows to look at data in different areas of a worksheet. This lets you look, for example, at the labels stored in the top rows of the worksheet while you also look at information

such as column totals stored at the bottom of the worksheet. 1-2-3 lets you split its display into *windows* that look at separate parts of the worksheet. You can split the worksheet screen in two halves, or windows, either vertically or horizontally. You can also choose the location on the worksheet where 1-2-3 makes the split. To create a window,

1. First move the cell pointer anywhere in the row (for a horizontal split) or column (for a vertical split) where you want the worksheet screen to divide into two windows. For example, to show rows 1 through 10 in the top window, move the cell pointer to a cell in row 11.

2. Type **/WW** to select the **/**Worksheet Window command.

3. When 1-2-3 displays the options for how your screen can be split, type **H** to select Horizontal or **V** to select Vertical. (For our example, choose **H**.)

As soon as you choose the Horizontal or Vertical option, 1-2-3 splits the worksheet screen into two windows at the current row or column. You can switch the cell pointer between the two windows by pressing the **F6** key (**WINDOW**).

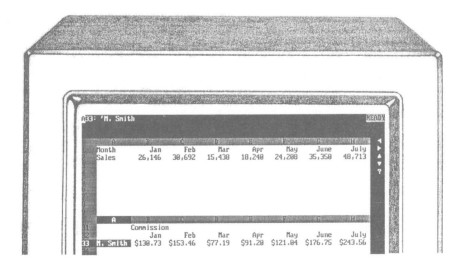

## /Worksheet Window Horizontal

This command splits the worksheet area into two windows starting at the cell pointer's row.

## /Worksheet Window Vertical

This command splits the worksheet area into two windows starting at the cell pointer's column.

While the windows are displayed, you can move about in either window to shift the part of the worksheet display that appears in that window. Using the default window settings, when you shift the contents in one window, 1-2-3 may shift the contents of the other. For example, in horizontal windows, shifting the contents of one window left or right also shifts the contents of the other window in the same direction, but 1-2-3 does not shift the other window's contents up or down. For vertical windows, shifting one window up or down also shifts the other window in the same direction, but 1-2-3 does not shift the other window left or right.

When you are finished with the window and want to again display a full-sized worksheet screen, type /WWC to select /Worksheet Window Clear. The second window disappears, and the top or left window fills the entire worksheet display area.

---

## /Worksheet Window Clear

This command removes the two horizontal or vertical windows so the worksheet fills up the display area.

---

# Keys to Success

1-2-3 lets you adjust the format and appearance of a worksheet so you can make the information you are presenting look better. The /Range Format command lets you format numeric entries and formula results. You can arrange a column so that its numbers line up according to their decimal point. You can also have 1-2-3 add formatting characters to numbers, such as $, %, or a comma separator. Use the /Range Label command to change the alignment for a range of labels. This is a timesaver because you don't have to edit each label in the range to change its label indicator.

You can also change column widths so that columns are wide enough to display long labels and formatted values. The /Worksheet Column-Width Set-Width command sets a single column to a width of 1 to 240 (511 in Release 3 and 3.1). You can enter the new column width by either typing it in or selecting it using the ARROW keys.

The /Worksheet Window commands let you split the worksheet area into two windows to look at different sections of the worksheet at the same time. You can split the worksheet into vertical or horizontal windows, switch between them, and then remove them when you are finished.

# What Do They Mean By . . . ?

Column-Width Indicator    An entry in square brackets next to the format indicator that displays the width selected for the column.

Format    To change the appearance of a number without changing its value.

Format Indicator    A parenthetical entry that appears on the control panel in front of a cell's contents and indicates the formatting applied to the cell.

Scientific Notation    A display format that presents a number as the power of ten you must multiply it by.

Windows    Halves of a worksheet (horizontal or vertical) that let you look at two sections of the worksheet simultaneously.

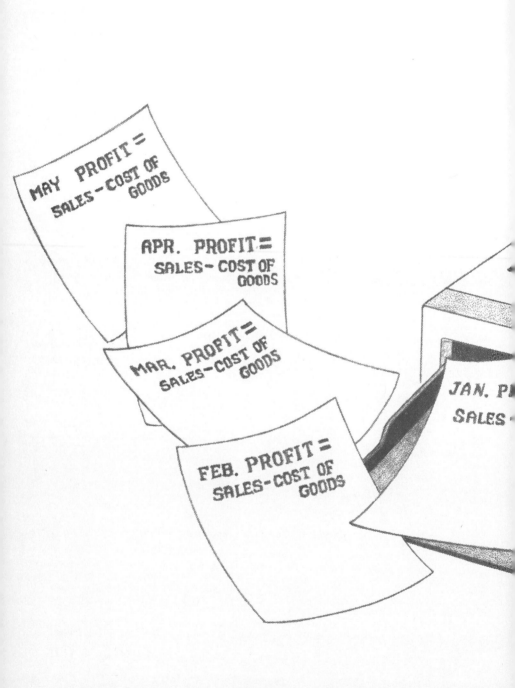

# Copying
# Worksheet
# Entries

One way to complete your worksheet models is to enter the contents of each cell, one by one, but you can do it more quickly by letting 1-2-3 repeat entries for you. For example, if you have a list of product parts in one part of the worksheet and you need that same list to appear elsewhere, letting 1-2-3 copy the product list is faster and less error prone than retyping it yourself.

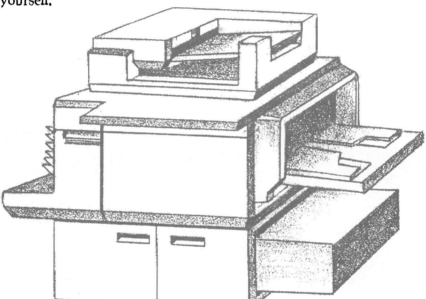

With the /Copy command, you can copy cell entries across rows or down columns; you can even copy entire ranges. Besides copying labels and numbers, you can also copy formulas. When you copy formulas, you really experience 1-2-3's power—you will learn in this chapter how 1-2-3 automatically adjusts a copied formula's references based on the formula's new location.

## Copying Labels and Values

Copying labels and values is easy, whether you copy one entry or 100 because 1-2-3 is just making an additional copy of an entry and putting it in another location. You can make one copy of a label or number or several copies—with one step. You can also copy an entire range of entries to another location. Besides copying the entries, 1-2-3 also copies any numeric format that you have assigned to them.

Be careful: Any existing entries in the cells to which you copy data will be overwritten with the copied data. In a copy operation, pick the new range carefully so you don't accidentally lose any cell entries that are already there.

## /Copy

This command takes existing entries and duplicates them in another location of the worksheet. After invoking the command, you select the cell or range to copy and press ENTER. Next, select the range containing the first cell of each copy to make and press ENTER.

## Copying One Cell Entry to Another Cell

Copying a label or value to another cell has the same effect as moving to the other cell and typing the entry a second time. The difference is that copying the entry requires less time than retyping it. To copy a cell,

1. In your practice worksheet, move the cell pointer to the entry you want to copy.

2. Type /C to select the /Copy command.

3. 1-2-3 prompts you for the cell address to copy and suggests the current cell's address. (The wording of this prompt will vary slightly depending on which release of 1-2-3 you are using, but in all cases, 1-2-3 wants you to tell it what cell you want to copy.) Since this is the cell you are copying, press ENTER.

4. Now 1-2-3 prompts for where you want the copy to be placed and again suggests the current cell's address. Since you do not want to copy the cell onto itself, move the cell pointer to the cell where you want the copy to appear. (Remember—pick a cell that doesn't contain data you want to keep.) Press ENTER again.

1-2-3 duplicates the cell entry just as if you had typed it again.

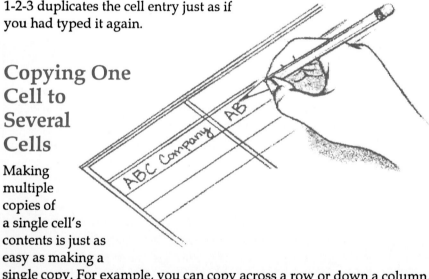

## Copying One Cell to Several Cells

Making multiple copies of a single cell's contents is just as easy as making a single copy. For example, you can copy across a row or down a column. To copy a cell's entry to multiple cells,

1. Move the cell pointer to the entry you want to copy.

2. Type /C to select the /Copy command.

3. 1-2-3 prompts you for the address of the cell to copy and shows the current cell in the input line. Since you are copying only the current cell, press ENTER.

4. Now 1-2-3 prompts for where you want the cell to be copied. Move the cell pointer to the first cell where you want the entry to appear. Since you're making multiple copies of the cell this time, you'll need to specify a range address. So type a period, and then move the cell pointer to the last cell in which you want the entry to appear. (Remember—pick a range that does not contain any data you want to keep.) Press ENTER again.

1-2-3 duplicates the entry in each cell of the range, just as if you had typed it again and again into each cell.

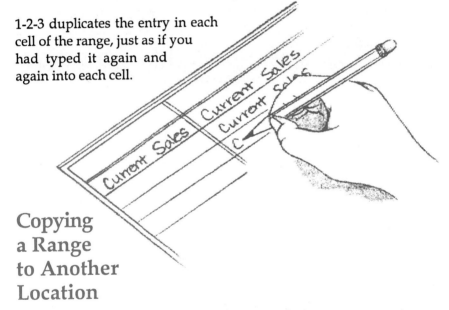

# Copying a Range to Another Location

You can also copy an entire range of entries—for instance, account names or months of the year—to another location on the worksheet. To copy a range,

1. Move the cell pointer to the first cell in the range you want to copy.

*Note: Although you can indicate a range address by specifying any two diagonally opposite corners, the upper-left cell typically is specified first.*

2. Type **/C** for the **/C**opy command.

3. When 1-2-3 prompts you for the entries to copy, move the cell pointer so the range includes all of the cells you want to copy. Press ENTER.

4. When 1-2-3 prompts you for the range to receive the copy, move the cell pointer to the first cell of this range. (Remember to make sure this area doesn't already contain important data.) Press ENTER.

Note that you don't need to select the full range address to receive the copy; 1-2-3 automatically copies each entry from the original range into a range

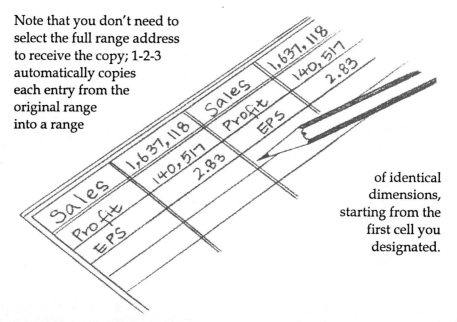

of identical dimensions, starting from the first cell you designated.

## Copying a Range to Multiple Locations

Another use of the /Copy command is for copying a range into multiple locations. For example, suppose you want to copy the entries in A1..A5 so they also appear in B1..B5, C1..C5, and D1..D5. Let's try this in your practice worksheet.

1. Move the cell pointer to the first cell in the range you want to copy, A1.

2. Type /C for the /Copy command.

3. When 1-2-3 prompts for the range to copy, move the cell pointer until the range address includes all the cells you want to copy—in our example, A1..A5. Press ENTER.

4. When 1-2-3 prompts you for the range to receive the copy, move the cell pointer to the first cell of that range—in our example, B1. Type a period to convert the cell address to a range address; then move the cell pointer to specify a range that includes *the first cell of each range you want to receive the copied range.* For our example, you want to copy into three ranges—B1..B5, C1..C5, and D1..D5—so the "Copy to" range must be B1..D1. (As always, remember to select an area of the worksheet that does not contain important data.) Press ENTER again.

1-2-3 makes three copies of the original range, with the same dimensions, starting in each cell of the "Copy to"

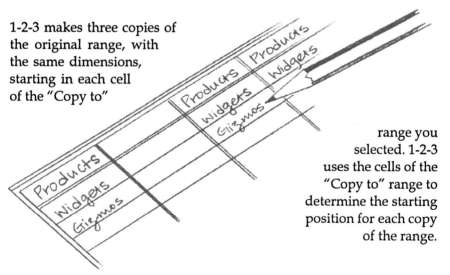

range you selected. 1-2-3 uses the cells of the "Copy to" range to determine the starting position for each copy of the range.

# Copying Formulas

So far you have learned to use the /Copy command to copy only labels and numbers. 1-2-3 can also copy formulas—with a slightly different result. When you copy a formula, 1-2-3 adjusts the cell references used in the formula to match the formula's new location. If you want, you also have the option of telling 1-2-3 not to adjust cell formulas when it copies them.

Copying a formula is just the same as copying labels and numbers: You can make one or many copies; and the formula can be the only entry you copy or it can be part of a range that includes other entries.

## Copying a Formula Several Times

To see how 1-2-3 copies formulas, let's try copying a simple formula. In your practice worksheet, make sure the formula +A1*A2 is stored in cell A3. (If you'd rather use another cell, that's fine.) To copy this formula into the range B3..D3 (or any other range of your choice), take the following steps:

1. Move the cell pointer to A3 (or whatever cell your formula is in) as the first entry to copy.

2. Type /C for the /Copy command.

3. In response to the prompt for the entry to copy, press ENTER.

4. In response to the prompt for the "Copy to" range, move to B3, type a period, and press the RIGHT ARROW twice. This specifies B3..D3 as the range where the entry should be copied. Press ENTER again.

1-2-3 puts three copies of your formula into cells B3, C3, and D3. Notice how the cell references in each copy are adjusted. In the next section, you'll learn more about these adjusted references.

### Understanding Relative References

Let's look more closely at the adjusted formulas in the previous example. To see the difference, press the RIGHT ARROW and LEFT ARROW to move through the entries on row 3. The formulas look like this:

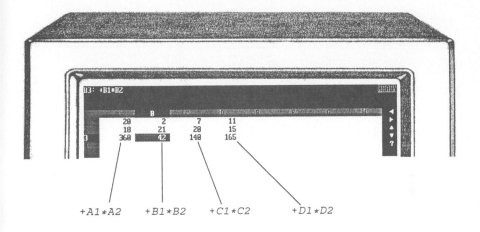

+A1*A2        +B1*B2        +C1*C2              +D1*D2

The cell addresses in the formula from A3 have been adjusted as the formula is copied to other cells in the row. This is because the cell address references in the original formula are *relative references*.

Relative references mean that 1-2-3 does not remember the exact addresses of the cells to use in a calculation, such as the cells A1 and A2 for the formula in A3. Rather, 1-2-3 remembers the cells to use in a formula by their *relative distance* from the cell that contains the formula. Thus for the formula in A3, 1-2-3 remembers to multiply the value two cells above it by the value one cell above it.

The effect of relative references becomes apparent when you copy formulas. 1-2-3 adjusts relative cell references in a copied formula so that *it refers to cells that are the same distance from it as the distance between the original formula and its cell addresses.* In our example, the results of these adjustments ensure that the formula in D3 also multiplies the value two cells above it by the value one cell above it—just like the formula in A3. The difference is that the formula in A3 uses values stored in A1 and A2, but the formula in D3 uses the values stored in D1 and D2.

| Sales | 1000000 | |
| Cost of good sold | 500000 | ← 50% of Sales |
| Gross Profit | 500000 | ← Sales minus Cost of goods Sold |
| Operating Expenses | 300000 | |
| Profit | 200000 | ← Gross profit minus Operating expenses |

Relative references come into play only when you copy a formula. Most of the time you will not be concerned with how the formula remembers what cells it needs to make its calculation.

## Creating a Model with Relative References

Let's create a model that uses relative references in formulas that are copied.

1. Press HOME to get the cell pointer into A1.

2. Make the following cell entries, starting in A1.

> Type **Sales Commissions** and press the DOWN ARROW.
> Type **Sales** and press the RIGHT ARROW.
> Type **Commissions** and press the DOWN ARROW, then the LEFT ARROW.
> Type **500000** and press the DOWN ARROW.
> Type **600000** and press the DOWN ARROW.
> Type **700000** and press the DOWN ARROW.
> Type **800000** and press the UP ARROW three times, then the RIGHT ARROW once.

3. You should now be in cell B3. Type **+A3\*.05** and press ENTER to create a formula that calculates commissions of 5 percent.

4. Type **/C** to select the **/**Copy command. Press ENTER to copy the current cell. To copy the formula into B4..B6, press the DOWN ARROW, type a period, press the DOWN ARROW twice, and press ENTER.

Your worksheet and the formulas now look like this:

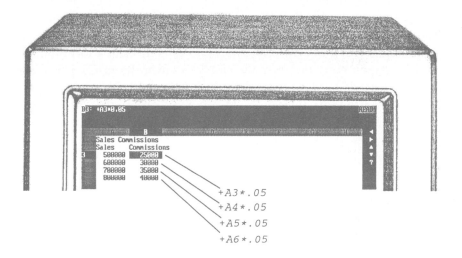

You may want to save this worksheet by typing **/FS** to select the **/**File Save command; then type a filename—such as SALES—and press ENTER. To erase the worksheet and bring up a blank worksheet to create the next model, type **/WEY** (**/**Worksheet Erase with a Yes confirmation).

## Copying Formulas Without Adjusting Cell References

There will be times when you'll want to copy a formula without having the formula's cell addresses adjusted. 1-2-3 has another type of cell reference, the *absolute reference*, that is used for cell addresses and range addresses that should not change when the formula is copied. A reference of this type allows you to use an unchanging value as part of your formula—for example, a commission percentage, interest rate, or salary increase amount that applies to several different computations.

To indicate that a cell or range address is an absolute reference, put a $ in front of both the column and row indicators in the cell address—as in $A$1. When 1-2-3 copies a formula, it does not adjust any absolute references in that formula. For example, $A$1 will remain $A$1 regardless of where you copy it to. 1-2-3 does not change these references since it remembers the absolute addresses that were used in the original formulas.

You can combine relative and absolute references in a formula; for example, if you copy the formula +B2*$A$3 from B5 to C5..D5, 1-2-3 adjusts the first cell address in the formula but does not change the second cell address. The two copies of the formula will become +C2*$A$3 and +D2*$A$3. 1-2-3 does not change the A3 reference because it is an absolute reference.

### Creating a Model with Absolute References

In the next exercise, you'll see what happens in a model that contains formulas with absolute references.

1. Bring the cell pointer into cell A2. Starting there, make the following entries:

> Type **Sales Projections** and press DOWN ARROW.
> Type **Growth** and press the RIGHT ARROW twice.
> Type **7.5%** and press the UP ARROW twice.
> Type **^1992** and press the RIGHT ARROW.
> Type **^1993** and press the RIGHT ARROW.
> Type **^1994** and press the RIGHT ARROW.
> Type **^1995** and press the DOWN ARROW once, then the
> LEFT ARROW three times.
> Type **100000** and press the RIGHT ARROW.

2. The cell pointer should be in cell D2. Type **+C2*(1+$C$3)** and press Enter to create a formula that calculates sales projections. These projections will all be based on the prior year's sales and a fixed percentage of increase equal to the number stored in C3.

3. Type **/C** to select the **/Copy** command.

4. To copy the formula from the current cell, press Enter.

5. To copy the formula into E2..F2, press the Right Arrow, type a period, press the Right Arrow, and press Enter again.

Your worksheet and the formulas now look like this:

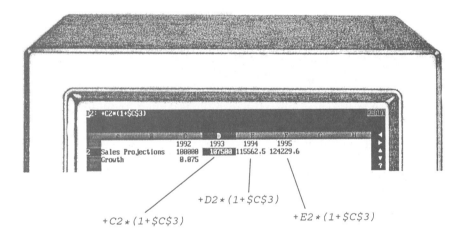

$$+D2*(1+\$C\$3)$$

$$+C2*(1+\$C\$3)$$

$$+E2*(1+\$C\$3)$$

# Keys to Success

Having 1-2-3 copy your entries—values, labels, and formulas—to other worksheet cells lets you quickly duplicate entries from one location to another. You can copy one cell to another, one cell into a range of cells, a range to another range, or a range into multiple copies of the range.

When you are copying numbers and labels, the result is the same as if you moved to the new location and typed the entries again. With formulas, 1-2-3 looks at the cell addresses in the formula and decides whether to adjust them or not depending on whether they are relative or absolute references. Relative references are adjusted so the cells referenced in the copy of the formula are the same relative distance from one another as the cells referenced in the original formula. 1-2-3 does not change absolute references in formulas.

# What Do They Mean By . . . ?

Absolute Reference    In a formula, this is a cell or range address (reference) that does not change when the formula is copied.

Relative Reference    In a formula, this is a cell or range address (reference) that is adjusted when the formula is copied to another location.

# Moving Entries

## 8

When you move into a new house or office or wish to rearrange a room, unpacking and arranging your furniture takes a lot of effort. With 1-2-3 worksheets, however, when you decide that a different organization of the information will help your reader understand the data, you can easily restructure the data without having to reenter it.

1-2-3's /Move command handles the changes for you, making the task of rearranging a worksheet easy. The /Move command not only relocates entries, including their formatting, but also keeps track of cell references in formulas, so they always reference the same data. The /Move command needs to know only the cell or range you want to move and where you want to move it. For example, you can take a worksheet that has all its entries grouped in the upper-left corner and spread them around to better use the workspace and improve readability.

# *Moving Labels and Values*

Moving labels and values to another location is just like cutting out the piece of ledger paper that contains the entries and pasting it in another location. To move a cell or range,

1. Move the cell pointer to the first cell you want to move.

2. Type **/M** for the **/M**ove command.

3. When 1-2-3 prompts you for the cells to move, move the cell pointer to highlight all the entries you want to move, and press ENTER.

4. When 1-2-3 prompts you for the new location for the range, move the cell pointer to the first cell where you want the range placed, and press ENTER again.

Like copying a range to another location, as you learned in Chapter 7, you don't need to select the exact dimensions of the  range to be moved. It will be the same size in its new location as it was in its previous one, beginning in the cell you selected in response to the /Move command's prompt for a new location.

# /Move

This command relocates entries to another spot in the worksheet. After selecting the command, specify the cell or range to move and press ENTER. Next, select the first cell of the new location to which you want the cell or range moved, and press ENTER again. If the moved entries have any numeric formatting, this is moved along with the entries.

## Moving Entries Within a Model

Let's create a model in which to practice the /Move command.

1. Press HOME so that the cell pointer is in A1. Make the following entries:

In A1, type **Salesperson** and press the RIGHT ARROW. Type **Sales** and press the RIGHT ARROW. Type **Commissions** and press the DOWN ARROW once and the LEFT ARROW twice to move to A2.

In A2, type **Johnson** and press the RIGHT ARROW. Type **600000** and press the RIGHT ARROW. Type **6530** and press the DOWN ARROW. Then press the LEFT ARROW twice to move to A3.

In A3, type **Smith** and press the RIGHT ARROW. Type **500000** and press the RIGHT ARROW. Type **5270** and press ENTER.

Your worksheet entries will look like this:

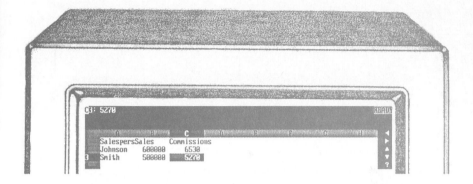

As you can see, the entries are too close together to be easily read. The column label in column A is too wide to fit in the default column width. You can change the entire appearance of the data by moving all the columns of entries. (Another way to handle the problem with the label in column A is to widen the column.) Now let's continue with our example model and use the /Move command to rearrange the columns.

2. Press the Up Arrow twice and the Left Arrow once to move to B1.

3. Type /M to select the /Move command.

4. To highlight the range B1..C3, press the Down Arrow twice and the Right Arrow once. Press Enter to complete the selection.

5. To move the highlighted entries to C1..D3, press the Right Arrow once, and then Enter.

6. Press the Right Arrow twice to move to D1.

7. Type /M to select the /Move command.

8. To specify D1..D3 as the range to be moved, press the Down Arrow twice, and then press Enter.

9. To move these entries to E1..E3, press the Right Arrow once, and then Enter.

Your worksheet now looks like this:

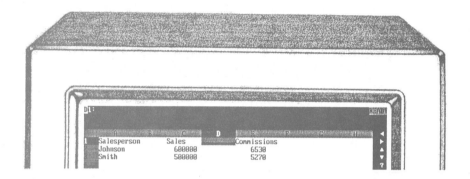

You may want to save this rearranged worksheet now by typing /**FS** to select the /File Save command. Enter a filename—such as SALECOMM— and press ENTER. Now you can type /**WEY** (/Worksheet Erase with a **Yes** confirmation) to erase the worksheet and get a new, empty one.

## *Moving Formulas*

You can use the /Move command to move formulas, too. Just use the same steps as you did for moving labels and numbers. Remember—1-2-3 adjusts cell addresses in formulas as they move so the formula always references the right data. And if you move the referenced cell itself, 1-2-3 changes the formula to reflect the new address. Thus if you have a formula that references a value of 10 stored in B2, and you move the 10 from B2 to IV100, 1-2-3 changes any formula referencing B2 to reference IV100 instead; the formula will still reference the same value, but in its new location.

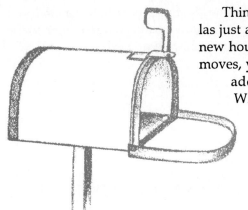

Think of moving entries and formulas just as you do a friend moving to a new house. When your friend Rebecca moves, you can contact her at her new address in a different location. When you contact your other friends, you continue to use their old addresses—they are not affected by Rebecca's address change.

# Moving Formulas in a Worksheet

To see how 1-2-3 adjusts formulas, try moving a few. First create a worksheet with several different formulas.

1. Enter these labels, pressing the RIGHT ARROW after each entry:

   Type **Clerk** in A1, **Yr Pay** in B1, **Wk Pay** in C1, **Bonus** in D1, and **Commiss** in E1.

2. Type **Sales** in F1 and press ENTER.

3. Press HOME and the DOWN ARROW to move to A2. In row 2, make the following entries, pressing the RIGHT ARROW after you type each cell's contents:

   Type **Smith** in A2, **+C2\*52** in B2, **300** in C2, **+E2\*.1** in D2, and **+F2\*.005** in E2.

4. Type **600000** in F2 and press ENTER.

Your worksheet now looks like the one illustrated next. In this model, you have entered the formulas as labels to allow you to compare them to the formulas after the move operation, which we'll do next.

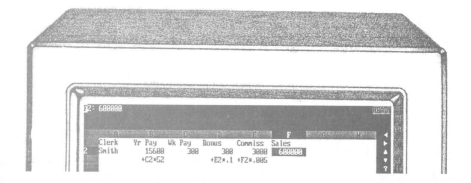

5. To move the formulas in C2..E2 to C5..E5, put the cell pointer in C2 as the first entry to move.

6. Type /M for the /Move command.

7. To highlight C2..E2 as the range to move, press the RIGHT ARROW twice, and press ENTER in response to the prompt.

8. Move to C5, the cell where you want 1-2-3 to begin to place the relocated entries, and press ENTER.

1-2-3 moves the formulas from C2..E2 to C5..E5, as shown here:

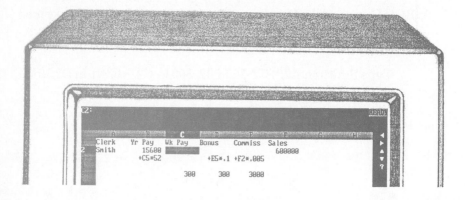

In the preceding illustration, notice the adjustments that 1-2-3 has made because of the move operation. The results of the formulas have not changed, because 1-2-3 adjusts every formula in the worksheet to use the new locations of the referenced cells. The following things have occurred:

- The formula for cell B2 changes from +C2*52 to +C5*52 because the value the formula uses (300) moved from C2 to C5.

- The formula for cell D5 changes from +E2*.1 to +E5*.1 because the value the formula uses (the result of the formula previously in E2) moved to E5.

- The formula for cell E5 does not change because the value it used (600000 stored in F2) has not moved, even though the formula has moved.

These types of *formula adjustments* occur regardless of whether cell addresses are relative or absolute references. When the cell references in formulas are changed by moving entries, those cell references remain relative or absolute, as they were before you moved the referenced cells.

## Keys to Success

With 1-2-3's /Move command, you can rearrange the data in a worksheet to best fit your needs. When you move labels and numbers, 1-2-3 cuts them from one location and pastes them elsewhere, without any change to the cells in their new location. If these numbers or labels are referenced by formulas, the formulas are updated to refer to the new locations—even though the formulas do not move. If you do move formulas, the formulas are adjusted as necessary when the data that they reference is relocated.

# *What Do They Mean By . . . ?*

**Formula Adjustment**  A change in a cell address within a formula to refer to the cell's new location.

**Move**  To relocate cell entries to a different location on the worksheet.

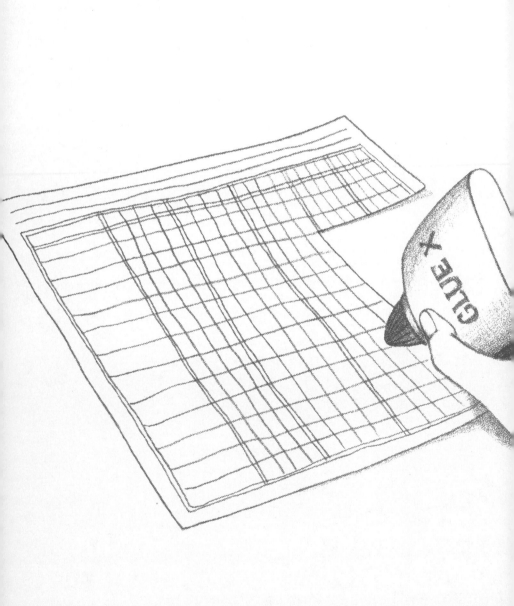

# Adding and Removing Entries

9

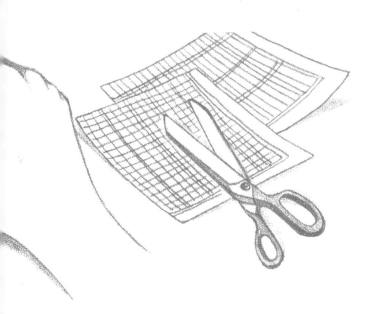

Besides copying and moving entries, another way to rearrange your worksheets is by *inserting* and *deleting* entire columns or rows. Inserting blank columns and rows is like moving blank rows or columns from somewhere in the worksheet and inserting them into another location. Deleting columns and rows is like cutting them out of the worksheet and then pasting together the remaining pieces.

When you delete columns and rows, the entries in the entire row or column you delete are permanently lost. You can also hide columns temporarily with all releases except 1A; they disappear from the display, but not from the worksheet itself. When you want the data to reappear, you can use another command to make this happen.

## Inserting Columns and Rows

When you want to add another row or column in the middle of your worksheet, you don't have to move all of the existing entries to make room for the new ones. Instead, you can have 1-2-3 insert the new columns or rows for you. Inserting new, blank columns or rows in a worksheet does not increase the maximum number of columns or rows available to you in the 1-2-3 worksheet; when you insert a blank column or row, it is supplied from the available blank ones.

### /Worksheet Insert

This command inserts blank columns or rows at the current cell location. After selecting the command, choose **Column** or **Row** to specify whether you want to add columns or rows. Next, specify a range that includes the number of columns or rows you want to add, and press ENTER. When 1-2-3 inserts the new columns or rows, it adjusts the cell references in any affected formulas to reflect the new locations.

# Inserting Columns

When you insert one or more columns in a worksheet, 1-2-3 cuts the columns from the right edge of the worksheet and moves them to the current location. The letters used to refer to these columns depend on the insert location and maintain 1-2-3's sequential lettering. Any formulas that reference data in columns to the right of the insert location will

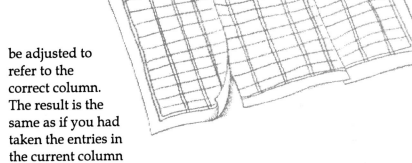

be adjusted to refer to the correct column. The result is the same as if you had taken the entries in the current column and the ones to its right and moved all of them one or more columns to the right. The difference is that an insert operation requires fewer steps than a move operation.

To insert a column, you first move the cell pointer to any cell in the column where you want the blank column to be inserted; that is, into the column that will become the new, blank column. Next, you invoke the /Worksheet Insert Column command. You'll then see this prompt:

Enter column insert range:

1-2-3 wants you to tell it how many columns you want to insert, and will insert the same number of columns as the range includes. If you want to insert only one column, just press ENTER. To insert two or more columns, press the RIGHT ARROW once for each column more than one that you want to insert.

# Inserting Rows

When you insert new rows in a worksheet, 1-2-3 takes one or more rows from the bottom of the worksheet, moves them to the current row, uses new row numbers for all rows below the inserted rows, and adjusts any affected formulas to refer to these new rows. You can accomplish this same alteration by moving everything down one row, leaving a blank row, but this takes longer than using an insert operation.

To insert blank rows, move the cell pointer to any cell in the row where you want the new rows inserted; that is, into the row that will become the new, blank row. Next, invoke the /Worksheet Insert Row command. 1-2-3 prompts you for a range to insert. Specify a range that includes as many rows as you want to insert. If you want to insert only one row, just press ENTER. To insert two or more rows, press the DOWN ARROW once for each row more than one that you want to insert.

# Creating a Model for
# Inserting Columns and Rows

By creating and practicing with a simple model, you can see how 1-2-3 adjusts the worksheet when you insert columns and rows. To create this model, do the following:

1. Type **ABC Company** in A2, **XYZ Company** in A3, and **Total** in A4.

2. Type**/WCS** to select /Worksheet Column Set-Width. In response to the prompt, type **15** and press ENTER.

3. Type "**Sales** in B1 and **Units Sold** in C1.

4. Type the formulas **+C2∗5** in B2, **+C3∗4** in B3, and **@SUM(B2,B3)** in B4; press ENTER.

5. Type **/C** to select the **/Copy** command. Press **ENTER** to select B4, and press the **RIGHT ARROW** and **ENTER** to copy the @SUM formula to C4.

6. Type **40000** in C2 and **50000** in C3, so the worksheet looks like this:

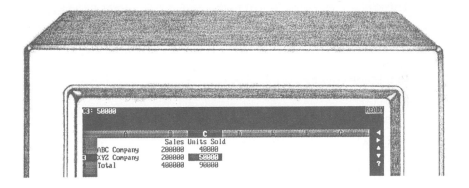

7. Now let's insert a blank column into this worksheet. With the cell pointer anywhere in column C, type **/WIC** to select **/Worksheet Insert Column**. When 1-2-3 prompts for a range to insert, press **ENTER** so the range contains only a single column. Your worksheet now looks like this:

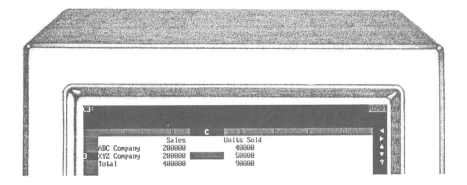

8. Let's take a look at the formulas that were affected by the addition of the blank column. Press the LEFT ARROW to move to B3. Notice that 1-2-3 changed the formula from +C3*4 to +D3*4. Press the DOWN ARROW once and the RIGHT ARROW twice to move to D4. Here, 1-2-3 adjusted the formula from @SUM(C2..C3) to @SUM(D2..D3). These changes are identical to the ones 1-2-3 would have made if you used the /Move command to move the entries in C1..C4 to D1..D4.

To insert a blank row into your worksheet, follow these steps:

1. Press the UP ARROW to move to any cell in row 3.

2. Type /WIR to select /Worksheet Insert Row. When 1-2-3 prompts for a range to insert, press ENTER so the range contains only one row. The worksheet with an inserted row looks like this:

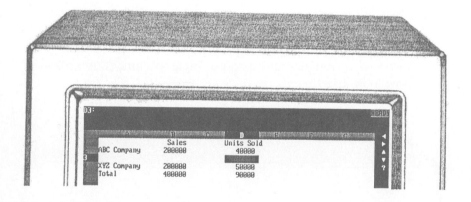

3. Press the DOWN ARROW. Notice how 1-2-3 expanded the range the @SUM function uses to include the row you inserted in the middle of the range. This is the same formula adjustment 1-2-3 would have made if you had used the /Move command to move A3..D4 to A4..D5.

Now, with the inserted blank column and row, you can add the entries for the new Smith company and the Cost column, so the completed model looks like this:

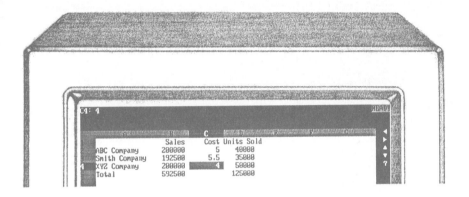

# Deleting Columns and Rows

When a column or row contains data you do not want, you have two choices. One way to get rid of the data is to move up all of the entries below it (to overwrite a row), or move left all of the entries to the right of it (to overwrite a column). Or, using fewer steps, you can delete the column or row itself.

*Warning: Deleting a column or row means you lose the data permanently, so— in case you change your mind or discover you made a mistake—you will want to save your worksheet before you make substantial deletions.*

When you delete columns or rows, you are not changing the size of the worksheet—all worksheets contain the same number of columns and rows. When you delete columns or rows, you are deleting them at the location you select and then adding the same number of empty columns or rows to the end of the worksheet.

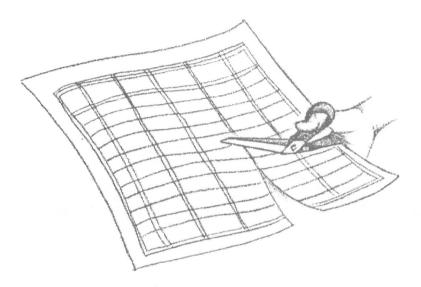

## /Worksheet Delete

This command removes columns or rows at the current cell location. After selecting the command, choose Column or Row to indicate whether you want to remove columns or rows. Next, select a range containing at least one cell from each column or row you want to remove, and press ENTER. When it deletes the range, 1-2-3 adjusts the cell references in any formulas affected by the deletion to reflect the cells' new locations.

# Deleting Columns

When you delete worksheet columns, you tell 1-2-3 to remove the columns from the current location, assign new letters to the columns to the right, relabel the columns, alter any formulas affected by the deletion, and add the same number of empty columns to the right edge of the worksheet. (You can also delete column entries without removing a column by erasing their contents with the /Range Erase command, or by moving a column from another location to overwrite the column you no longer want, with the /Move command.)

To delete one or more columns, move the cell pointer to any cell in the first column that you want to delete. Select the /Worksheet Delete Column command. Just as in an insert operation, 1-2-3 prompts you for a range to delete and will delete every column that is included in the range. To delete one entire column, you need only to specify one cell from that column as the range to delete, so just press ENTER in response to the prompt. To delete two or more columns, press the RIGHT ARROW once for each column more than one that you want to delete.

# Deleting Rows

When you delete rows from a worksheet, you tell 1-2-3 to remove one or more rows from the worksheet, assign new row numbers to rows beneath the deleted row, alter any formulas affected by the deletion, and add the same number of empty rows to the bottom of the worksheet.

To delete one or more rows, move the cell pointer to any cell in the first row you want to delete. Select the /Worksheet Delete Row command. 1-2-3 next displays the usual prompt for a range to delete, and will delete as many rows as are included in the range you select. To delete one entire row, you need only to specify one cell from that row as the range to delete, so just press ENTER in response to the prompt. To delete two or more rows, press the DOWN ARROW for each row more than one that you want to delete.

## An Exercise in Deleting Columns and Rows

By using the same simple model that you used to practice insert operations, you can see how 1-2-3 adjusts the worksheet when you delete columns and rows.

1. To delete a column from this worksheet, move the cell pointer into column C. Type /WDC to select /Worksheet Delete Column. When 1-2-3 prompts for a range to delete, press ENTER to delete only the single column C. The worksheet after you delete the column looks like this:

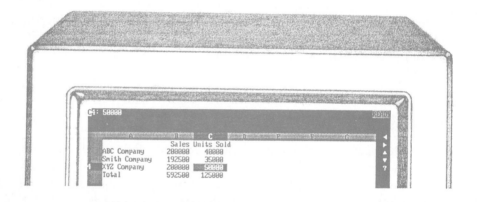

2. Move the cell pointer to B2. Notice that the formula is now +C3*4, just as if you moved the range D1..D4 over into C1..C4. The entries that were in column C have been permanently removed.

3. Now let's delete a row from the worksheet. Press the DOWN ARROW to move the cell pointer anywhere in row 3. Type /WDR to select /Worksheet Delete Row. When 1-2-3 prompts for a range to delete, press ENTER to delete only one row. The worksheet now looks like this:

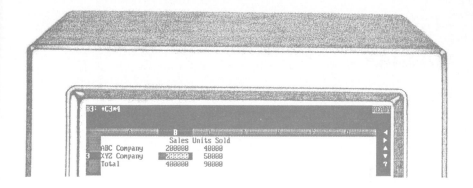

4. Press the **DOWN ARROW**. Notice how 1-2-3 contracted the range the @SUM function uses, because the row you deleted is in the middle of the range. 1-2-3 would have made the same formula adjustment if you had moved A4..C5 to A3..C4.

*Note: If you delete a column or row that a formula explicitly uses, 1-2-3 replaces the cell address with ERR. To see this, move the cell pointer into column C of the sample worksheet, type /WDC, and press* ENTER *to delete the current column. Since you have deleted a column that formulas reference, 1-2-3 replaces the cell references with ERR. Press the* LEFT ARROW *to move to B3, and notice the formula there. The formula reads +ERR*4, as shown here:*

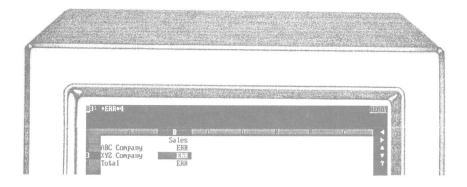

# Hiding Columns on the Worksheet Display

With ledger paper, if you don't want a specific column to be visible, you can fold the paper over so the column no longer appears. When you want to see the hidden column again, you unfold the paper. 1-2-3 (except Release 1A) lets you do the same thing. You can hide columns so they do not appear on the display of the worksheet, and you can add them back into the display when you want to. As on the ledger paper, your hidden 1-2-3 data is not lost. The data in hidden worksheet columns is still available to you, and formulas in those hidden cells are updated as usual.

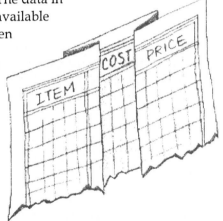

If you print your worksheet while columns are hidden, the hidden columns will not be printed. This is a good way to limit the printout of a worksheet and prevent certain columns from being seen in hard copy as well as on the screen.

To hide a column in the worksheet you've been working with in this chapter, select the /Worksheet Column Hide command (type / WCH). When 1-2-3 prompts you for a range of cells to hide, select at least one cell from each column you want to hide, and press ENTER. You can hide multiple columns, but only if they are adjacent. If you want to hide several scattered columns, you'll have to use separate / WCH commands. A worksheet with two columns hidden might look like this on the screen:

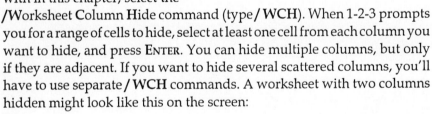

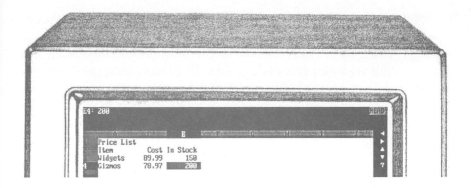

Remember—hidden worksheet columns are still available to you on the display. When you are using any command that expects you to specify a range of cells, 1-2-3 will be in POINT mode for selecting and will show the hidden columns of a worksheet. The hidden columns are displayed with asterisks next to the column letter, like this:

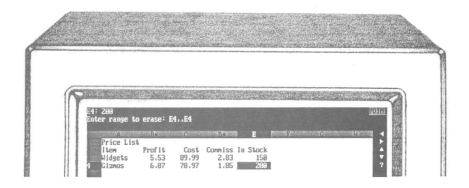

The asterisks will disappear when you leave POINT mode, and the columns will again disappear from view.

Let's try this on the worksheet you've been using. Type /RE to select the /Range Erase command, a command that will expect you to provide a range. You'll be in POINT mode, so the columns you've hidden will appear, with asterisks; press ENTER, and the hidden columns disappear again. If you include the hidden columns in the range you specify for the /Range Erase command, the contents of these columns included in the range will be erased along with the contents of visible columns.

## /Worksheet Column Hide

This command removes columns from the worksheet display—without removing the data from the worksheet. After selecting the command, specify a range containing at least one cell from each column you want to hide, and press ENTER. When you are in POINT mode for any command, the hidden columns will reappear with asterisks.

## Redisplaying Hidden Columns

On ledger paper, when you want to see the hidden columns, you can pull the edge of the paper to display the data hidden in the paper fold. With 1-2-3, you use the /Worksheet Column Display command. On your practice worksheet, type /WCD to select the command. 1-2-3 switches to POINT mode to prompt you for the range to display, so you can see the hidden columns with asterisks next to their letters. Specify a range that includes one cell from each of the hidden columns you want to display, and press ENTER.

*Tip:* With the /Worksheet Column Display command, you can include unhidden columns in the range you specify. So it's easy to redisplay multiple columns that are not adjacent—with just one /WCD command.

## /Worksheet Column Display

This command redisplays columns that have been hidden using the /Worksheet Column Hide command. After selecting the command, specify a range containing at least one cell from each hidden column you want to redisplay, and press ENTER. The range you specify can include unhidden columns.

# Keys to Success

In addition to moving data around to rearrange your worksheet, you can also insert and delete blank columns and rows. When you insert or delete columns and rows, 1-2-3 adjusts the formulas in the worksheet to reflect the new locations of any cell references that have been affected. For the /Worksheet Insert Column and /Worksheet Insert Row commands, specify a range that includes the number of columns or rows you want to add. For the /Worksheet Delete Column and /Worksheet Delete Row commands, specify a range that includes at least one cell from each column or row you want to remove.

You can also hide columns temporarily in the worksheet display without removing the data in the columns. To hide columns, use /Worksheet Column Hide and select a range containing cells from the columns to hide; you can hide several columns as long as they are adjacent. When you want to display hidden columns again, select the /Worksheet Column Display command and specify a range containing cells from the hidden columns. Hidden columns are also visible temporarily when you are in POINT mode for any command.

# What Do They Mean By . . . ?

Insert     To add a new blank column or row to a worksheet in the middle of the worksheet data.

Delete     To remove an entire column or row from the middle of the worksheet data. The entries in deleted rows and columns are permanently lost.

Hide     To temporarily remove columns from the worksheet display.

POINT Mode     A 1-2-3 mode for selecting a range used by 1-2-3 commands. You can use the Arrow keys to "point" to the range you want to select while in POINT mode.

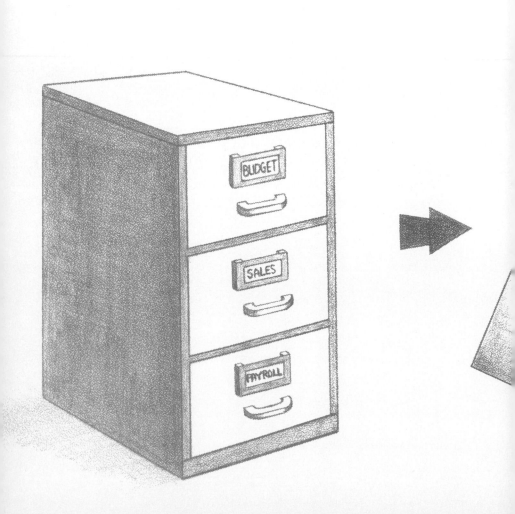

# *Looking at File Storage*

# 10

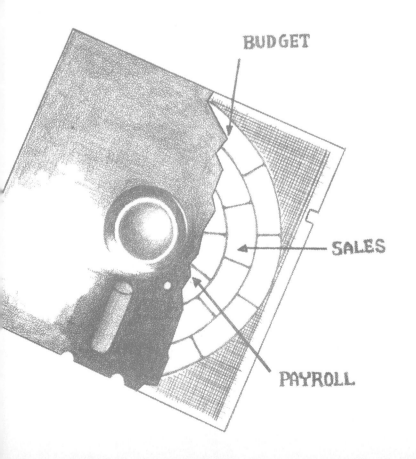

BUDGET

SALES

PAYROLL

137

The operating system on your computer, DOS, is in charge of storing the files that hold your data. When you retrieve a file, 1-2-3 uses DOS to get the file. When you save a file, 1-2-3 tells the operating system to save it with a name you provide. Since 1-2-3 handles sending and receiving the information, you do not need to know every detail about what the operating system is doing. When you want to use a file, you only need to know its name, and DOS will find it for you. You will want to build your knowledge base about files since they represent your investment of time as you work with your system.

DOS places the files you save on a *disk*. (This chapter focuses on *hard disk* file storage, but you can also save your files on *floppy disks*.) This is just like using a filing cabinet to store all of your papers. However, if you continue to place files in the drawer in random order as you create them, regardless of their content, filling up one drawer after another, as papers accumulate it will become more and more difficult to find the ones you want.

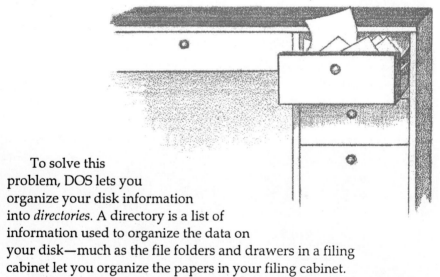

To solve this problem, DOS lets you organize your disk information into *directories*. A directory is a list of information used to organize the data on your disk—much as the file folders and drawers in a filing cabinet let you organize the papers in your filing cabinet.

When you use 1-2-3, you can create as many directories as you need to organize your models and tell 1-2-3 to change directories as you need files contained elsewhere. You can set 1-2-3 to automatically use a specific directory every time you boot up. You can also use 1-2-3 to view the list of files in a directory. When you no longer need a file, you can erase it from the disk.

## Organizing Your Disk

You will want to organize the files of information on your disk into directories, just as you use section dividers and file folders to organize the papers in your file cabinet. Then when you list a directory, you can see what it contains. If you are using 1-2-3 on a hard disk, information about your 1-2-3 files is stored in a 1-2-3 directory. This 1-2-3 directory lets you separate your worksheet files from your word processing, database, and other files.

You might also think of a disk and its directories as you do a tree with many branches. Any of the main branches may

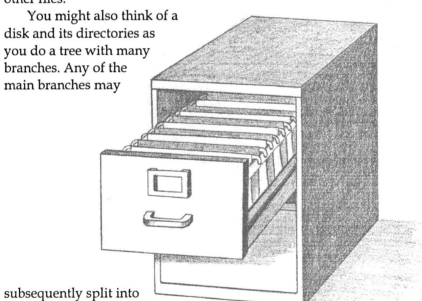

subsequently split into other branches, just as a directory may contain other directories (called *subdirectories*). For example, you might have directories called BUDGET and SALES in your 1-2-3 directory, and each of these directories might contain subdirectories named 1STQTR90,

JULY1990, and so forth. The files you store in any directory are like the tree's leaves, which can be on its main trunk or any of its multiple branches.

DOS has some rules you'll need to follow in creating your directories and files. One restriction is that every entry in a directory must

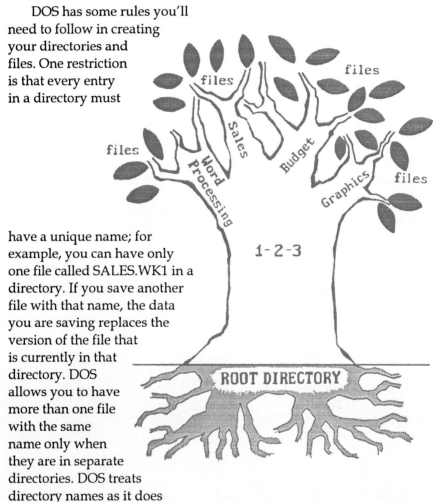

files

files

files

files

Sales

Word Processing

Budget

Graphics

1-2-3

ROOT DIRECTORY

have a unique name; for example, you can have only one file called SALES.WK1 in a directory. If you save another file with that name, the data you are saving replaces the version of the file that is currently in that directory. DOS allows you to have more than one file with the same name only when they are in separate directories. DOS treats directory names as it does filenames, so you cannot have a file called SALES if you have a directory called SALES. DOS also distinguishes filenames by their extensions, so you can have three separate files called SALES, SALES.WK1, and SALES.PIC.

Another DOS restriction controls the number of files the *root* directory (the main directory on the disk) may contain. Only root directories have a maximum allowable number of files—112, 224, or 512, depending on the disk size. If you try creating more files than the root directory allows, you will get a message that 1-2-3 cannot create the file.

## Understanding Path Names

DOS identifies each file by its disk drive and directory locations, and by its filename. The combination of these identifiers is called the file's *path*, that is, the path DOS must follow to find the file.

The path name starts with the drive letter followed by a colon, and then the directory names starting with the root directory. The subdirectories are listed in order as they fall under the root directory, separated by backslashes (\). The filename is also included in the path. Thus a file in the 123 directory on drive C has a path of C:\123, followed by the name of the file. The path for a file named AUG1991.WK1 in a subdirectory called SALES under the 1-2-3 subdirectory is C:\123\SALES\AUG1991.WK1.

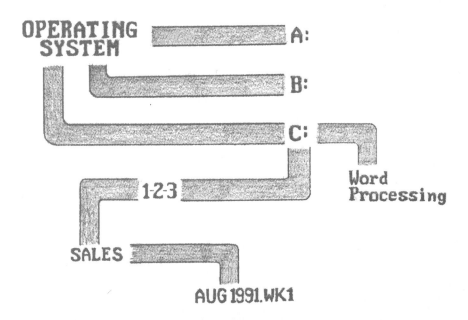

## Creating DOS Directories

Some of the directories on your disk are created by the programs you install. You will also want to create your own directories to use with 1-2-3 and other programs for storing and organizing your files.

To create directories, you use the DOS Make Directory (MD) command; to enter this command, you must exit 1-2-3 to get to the DOS command line. Let's try this. At the DOS prompt, type **MD**, followed by a space, and then the path of the directory you want to create. Press **ENTER** to execute the command.

Consider these two examples of MD commands:

   **MD \123\SALES**
   **MD A:\SALES**

- *Specifying the Drive*: DOS creates the directory named in the first example, \123\SALES, on the *current drive*. Or you can specify another drive, as in the second example, where the directory is created on the floppy disk drive A.

- *Specifying the Directory:* To create your new directory as a subdirectory of the root directory, start the path name with a \. If you do not start with \, DOS creates your new directory as a subdirectory of the current directory. So—if you're in the \ directory, and you enter the command **MD SALES**, DOS creates a directory path of C:\SALES. On the other hand, if you're in C:\123R23 as the current directory and you enter **MD SALES**, DOS creates a directory path of C:\123R23\SALES.

---

## DOS MD Command

This command creates a directory. After typing **MD**, enter the path for the directory you want to create and press Enter.

---

# *Using Directories with 1-2-3*

Once you have created directories for your 1-2-3 files, you can use 1-2-3 commands to tell the program how to use these directories. For example, you can specify a directory for the execution of an individual command, or you can tell 1-2-3 that you want to use the same directory for every command you enter in the entire 1-2-3 session.

## Changing the Directory for Your 1-2-3 Files

If you want to use a specific directory for all your worksheet files, you will need to tell 1-2-3 to use this directory for all of the commands you enter that use files—that is, as the *default current* directory. To do this, use the /File Directory command.

When you type **/FD** to select this command, 1-2-3 displays this message in the control panel:

```
  Enter current directory:
```

In response to this prompt, type the path where you want to store your files, and then press ENTER. 1-2-3 will then use this directory for saving and retrieving your worksheet files until you end your 1-2-3 session.

*Caution: If you are designating a floppy disk drive with the /FD command, make sure there is a disk in the drive, since 1-2-3 will read both the existing default directory setting and the directory that you specify as the new default directory before it makes a change.*

## /File Directory

This command sets the default current directory that 1-2-3 uses when it saves and retrieves files. After selecting this command, type the path for the directory you want to use and press ENTER.

# Changing the Directory for a Single Command

In addition to specifying the default directory, you may want to sometimes change the directory for a single command; you can do this in all 1-2-3 releases except 1A. For example, you might be systematically using files stored on your hard disk, but then need to work with a specific file on drive A before continuing to work in your default directory. To change the directory for a single /File Save or /File Retrieve command, simply enter the full path information when the command prompts you for the filename to save or retrieve.

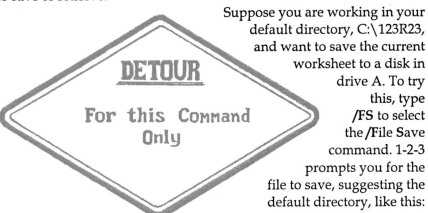

Suppose you are working in your default directory, C:\123R23, and want to save the current worksheet to a disk in drive A. To try this, type /FS to select the /File Save command. 1-2-3 prompts you for the file to save, suggesting the default directory, like this:

```
Enter name of file to save: C:\123R23\*.WK1
```

To change this path, press Esc two or three times until the suggested path information is completely removed. Next, type the new path (specifying drive A), a backslash, and the filename for the file you are saving—for example:

**A:\RICHARDS\BUDGET**

Finally, press ENTER, and 1-2-3 will save the file in the location you have specified.

By using a specific path with the /File Retrieve command, you can ask 1-2-3 to list the files in another location. To try this, type /FR to select the /File Retrieve command; 1-2-3 displays a list of files in the current directory. At the prompt for the name of the file to retrieve, press Esc two or three times until the suggested path information is removed. Then type the path for the directory of files you want to see, and press ENTER. 1-2-3 lists the files in the new location, ready for your selection.

# Listing Files in 1-2-3

As you use your files in 1-2-3, you may want to know more about them. DOS maintains several items of information about each file, including its name, its size (in bytes), and the date and time the file was last saved. There are two ways to see this information.

One way is a full-screen display of the file information, available through the /File List command. Try this command now: Type /FL, and select from several options for the type of files you want to list. Notice the options for Worksheet and Other. Worksheet displays the worksheet files in the current directory. The Other option displays all of the files in the current directory.

After you select an option, 1-2-3 presents the display you see at the top of the next page for the files you specified.

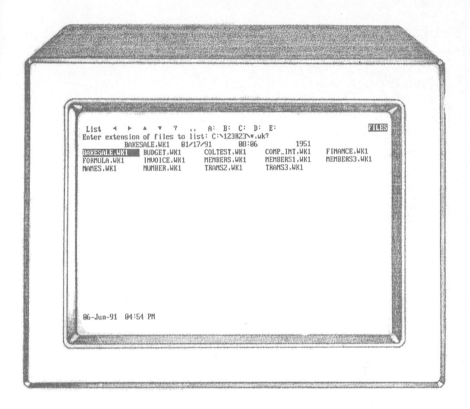

```
 List  ◄  ►  ▲  ▼  ?  ,,  A:  B:  C:  D:  E:                              FILES
 Enter extension of files to list: C:\123R23\*.wk?
            BAKESALE.WK1   01/17/91        00:06           1951
 BAKESALE.WK1       BUDGET.WK1      COLTEST.WK1     COMP_INT.WK1    FINANCE.WK1
 FORMULA.WK1        INVOICE.WK1     MEMBERS.WK1     MEMBERS1.WK1    MEMBERS3.WK1
 NAMES.WK1          NUMBER.WK1      TRANS2.WK1      TRANS3.WK1




 06-Jun-91   04:54 PM
```

Within this display, you can press the ARROW keys to move from filename to filename. Watch the control panel, where 1-2-3 displays the highlighted file's name, size, and last save information. When you press ENTER, 1-2-3 returns to READY mode.

You may need to display 1-2-3's file information about the files in the current directory before you retrieve a specific worksheet. Let's see how this works. Type **/FR** for the **/**File Retrieve command, and press **F3** (NAME); the main worksheet screen disappears. On line 3 of the control panel, you'll see the same file information that you get with the **/**File List command, followed by a list of the files in the current directory. This lets you select a file and view its file information when you need to see it before you retrieve the worksheet. When you're ready, just press ENTER to retrieve the worksheet whose file information you have displayed.

## /File List

This command lists information for the files in the current directory. After selecting this command, choose Worksheet to list worksheet files, or Other to list all files. Next, highlight the name of the file whose information you want to view. You'll see the file's name, size, and the date and time the file was last saved. Press ENTER to return to the READY mode.

# Erasing Files in 1-2-3

As you add and work with 1-2-3 worksheets, you will sometimes need to erase files you no longer need so that they do not take up valuable space on your disk. In all releases except 1A, you can use the /File Erase command to do this.

The /File Erase command is different from the /Worksheet Erase command. You will remember that the /Worksheet Erase command (Chapter 3) removes the worksheet data from 1-2-3's memory—without affecting any copy of the worksheet data on disk—so you can later bring the data back into 1-2-3 by retrieving the worksheet file. In contrast, /File Erase actually removes the worksheet data from the disk permanently.

The /File Erase command includes options for selecting the type of file to erase. To try this command, type /FE, and choose the type of file you want to erase, such as Worksheet for worksheet files or Other for any file. After you choose a file type, 1-2-3 displays all the files of the selected type in the current directory. To select a file to erase, either highlight its name in the list or type the filename in the control panel. Then press ENTER, and 1-2-3 displays a confirmation prompt. When you are certain you want to delete the file, select Yes to confirm your request, and 1-2-3 executes the file erasure. (Selecting No cancels the /File Erase command.)

**Erasing Files in Version 1A**    To erase a file in 1-2-3 version 1A, use the DOS Delete (DEL) command at the DOS command line. Type **DEL**, the path, and the filename of the file to erase; for example:

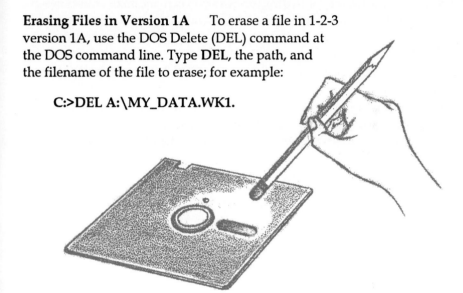

    **C:>DEL A:\MY_DATA.WK1.**

# /File Erase

This command removes a file permanently from a disk. After selecting this command, choose Worksheet to erase a worksheet file or Other to erase another type of file. Highlight the filename in the list or type the name of the file you want to erase, and press ENTER. Select Yes to confirm your request.

# Keys to Success

A disk can be divided into directories so you can organize your files—for example, by functions such as Sales or Accounting, or by software such as 1-2-3 or word processing. Each directory can contain other subdirectories and files. The main directory in the directory hierarchy of a disk is called the root (\) directory. You can use the DOS MD command to create directories.

1-2-3 can store your worksheet data in any location. Use the /File Directory command to do this; then specify the location for the file, and press ENTER. You can also designate a new location for a file with the /File Save and /File Retrieve commands.

The /File List command lists the name, size, and date and time of the last save for the files in a specific directory. You can also display this information by selecting /File Retrieve and pressing F3 (NAME).

When you want to permanently remove a file you have created, use the /File Erase command.

# What Do They Mean By . . . ?

Current or Default Directory   The drive and directory where 1-2-3 will store and look for worksheet files unless you provide another location. 1-2-3 looks in this location first.

Directory   A list of files on a disk.

Path   The drive and directory location of a file.

Root Directory   The main directory on all disks, signified by the name \.

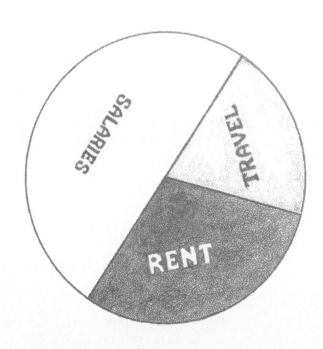

MAJOR BUDGET EXPENSES

# *Graphing Your Worksheet Data*

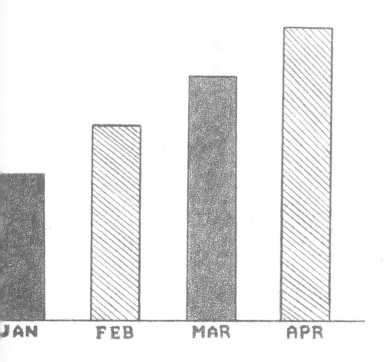

1-2-3 will display your models graphically, letting you show the essence of your data at a glance. A graph of numbers can show a trend or pattern that may not be apparent in a spreadsheet-style report using the same numbers. Since 1-2-3's graphs use the data you have already entered in worksheet cells, you can easily create your graphs by entering just a few commands.

In this chapter you will learn how to set up the data for a graph and how to create, display, enhance, and print a graph.

# Creating a Graph

All of 1-2-3's settings for creating and customizing graphs are in the menu for the /Graph command, as shown here:

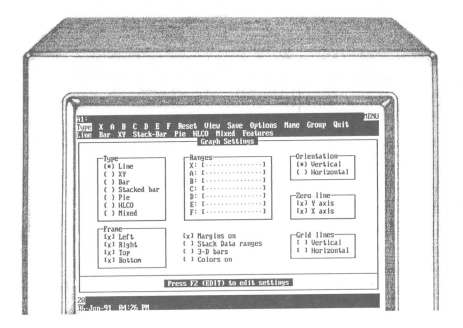

The Graph menu is sticky, so you must use the /Graph Quit command when you want to return to READY mode. As with the Print menu, 1-2-3 Releases 2.2, 2.3, and 3.1 display a settings sheet or dialog box that presents the settings you need to make a graph.

As you create the graph, you will not see any difference on the related worksheet; graph settings only affect the graph, not the worksheet data. To save a graph for the next time you use the worksheet, use the /File Save command as usual, and 1-2-3 saves both the worksheet data and the graph settings in the worksheet file.

## /Graph Quit

This command leaves the sticky main Graph menu and returns to the READY mode.

## About the X-axis and Y-axis

Most graphs have an *x-axis* and a *y-axis*. The x-axis is the horizontal line at the bottom of the graph; this line is divided into increments to show

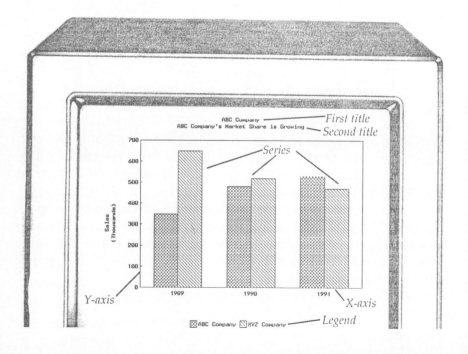

different data at each marked point. X-axis values may be numbers, but often are labels, dates, and other types of nonnumeric information. For example, if you are graphing sales for different divisions, the names of the divisions might be the x-axis values.

The y-axis is a vertical line at the left edge of the graph; this line displays a numeric scale for measuring the value of each x-axis data point. For example, suppose you are graphing sales data for the divisions of a company. The height of bars on the x-axis representing each division's sales might be measured against the total company sales numbers represented on the y-axis. 1-2-3 creates the y-axis for you, based on the values you specify for the graph.

## *Selecting the Data to Graph*

A graph can contain any type of numeric data. The worksheet data is organized into groups of related values, called *series*. Examples of data series are units sold in a region, or annual sales for a division over several years. A series is stored in a range of cells in a column or row of the worksheet. You can include up to six series—named A through F—in a single graph. Each series in the graph is distinguished by a different color or *hatch pattern*. The vertical bars in the preceding illustration represent the worksheet's data series.

To tell 1-2-3 that you want to use a range of the worksheet for a series, select the /Graph command and choose a letter A through F from the main Graph menu. Then specify the range by moving to the first cell, typing a period, moving to the last cell, and pressing ENTER.

You must also select the labels or values from the worksheet to be used along the x-axis, for example, the year labels in the preceding illustration. To do this, select the /Graph X command and specify the worksheet entries that you want to appear at the marked points of the x-axis. The graph's x-axis labels will include any formatting that the worksheet entries use.

## /Graph A through F

Use this command to select the worksheet values that the graph displays in each of its data series (up to six). After selecting a letter **A** through **F** from the main Graph menu, specify the range containing the values to graph and press ENTER.

## /Graph X

Use this command to select the worksheet entries displayed at the marked points of the graph's x-axis. After selecting this command, specify the range containing the entries and press ENTER.

# *Selecting the Graph Type*

You have probably seen many different types of graphs; graphed data can be shown as bars, pies, lines, and many combinations of these and other effects. 1-2-3 offers you several ways to graph your data, and each type of graph display works best for a specific kind of data. You may want to try all the different graph types with a worksheet to see the effect of each one.

You'll select a graph type with the /Graph Type command. When you invoke this command, 1-2-3 displays a selection of graph types from which you can choose; some of these are described in the box "Simple

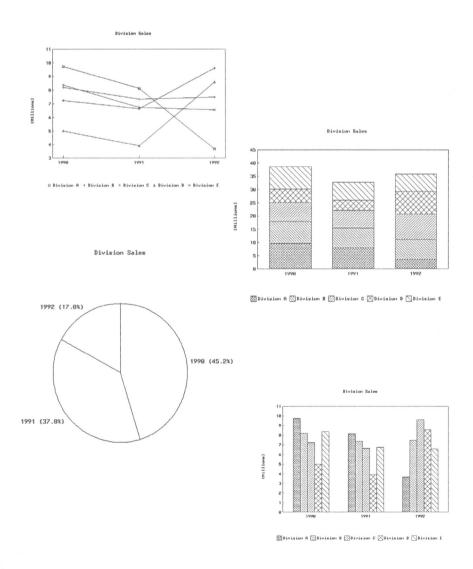

Graph Types." If you do not select a graph type, 1-2-3 will display your data as a line graph.

## Simple Graph Types

You will probably use these graph types most frequently:

- *Bar*  Each series in a bar graph is represented by bars with the same color or hatch pattern. The height of each bar is determined by the values in the series.

- *Line*  Each series is represented by its own string of symbols, and the symbols are connected by a line. The distance from the x-axis to each symbol on the line is a value in the series.

- *Pie*  This graph plots only one series, series A. The graph shows a pie in which each pie slice represents a value in the series. The size of each slice shows the proportion of that value to the series total.

- *Stacked Bar*  Each series is represented by bars with the same color or hatch pattern. The bars are stacked on top of one another as segments of a larger column, rather than placed next to one another as they are in a regular bar chart. The height of each segment of the stacked column for a series is determined by the values in that series.

## /Graph Type

Use this command to choose the format for 1-2-3 to use in graphing the data in your worksheet. After selecting the command, you can choose between Line, **XY**, Pie, Bar, and Stacked Bar.

# Showing the Graph

Once you have defined and selected your data and chosen how you want the data graphed, you will want to see how your data looks in this arrangement. To display a graph on the screen, use the /Graph View command. 1-2-3 displays your graph with all of the current settings you have made in the /Graph main menu (you'll learn more about these settings as you work through this chapter). Press any key, and 1-2-3 returns you to where you were before you displayed the graph.

Another option for viewing a graph is to select /Graph Quit to return to READY mode and then press **F10** (GRAPH) from the worksheet. As with the /Graph View command, 1-2-3 displays the current graph and then removes it from the screen when you press any key.

*Note: 1-2-3 can only display a graph if you have a graphics-capable display and if you selected the correct display when you installed 1-2-3. If your monitor cannot display graphs, you will not see them as you create them, but you can still create and print them.*

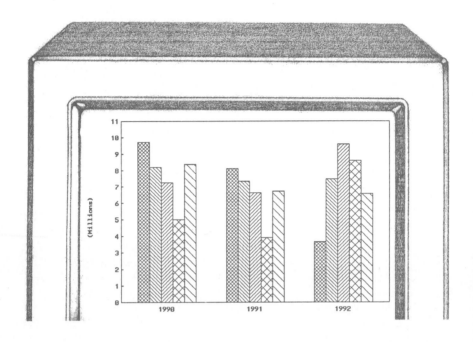

## /Graph View

This command displays the current graph using the current /Graph command settings. When you press any key, 1-2-3 returns you to the screen where you invoked the /Graph View command. You can also display the graph from the worksheet in READY mode by pressing **F10** (GRAPH). In 1-2-3 Releases 2.2 and later, you can also press **F10** (GRAPH) during other operations, such as in MENU mode.

# Adding Text to a Graph

The simplest graph, like the preceding one, represents only the worksheet values in the graph format you have chosen; this plain graph may not portray your model as well as you'd like. It may be difficult to understand because it includes no explanatory information about the data it is presenting. A viewer won't know if the graph is displaying sales figures, profit amounts, units sold, or budget overruns; nor will it be clear what each series of data represents. Adding text to your graphs lets you clarify their content.

The text at the top of the graph and along the two axes are the *graph titles*, and the group of boxes and text at the bottom, identifying the data series, is called the *legend*. You add this text to your graph using the /Graph Options command. In addition to options for text, this menu includes other advanced options that let you customize the graph, but these are beyond the scope of this book. The /Graph Options menu is a sticky menu, so when you want to return to the main Graph menu, select **Quit**.

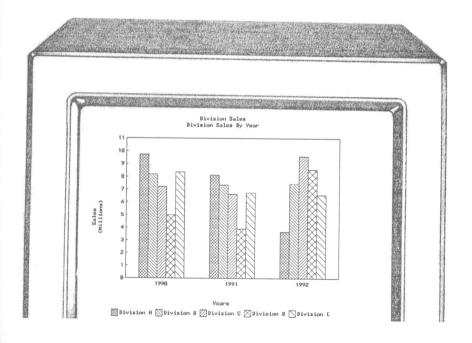

# Adding Graph Titles

There are four locations where you will frequently add explanatory text to a 1-2-3 graph: two lines of text at the top of the graph, a horizontal line next to the x-axis, and a vertical line next to the y-axis. To add text, select /Graph Options Titles. In the menu that follows, choose the location for the text (First, Second, X-Axis, or Y-Axis). Then type the text you want for that title and press ENTER.

## /Graph Options Titles

This command lets you enter explanatory text for the two titles at the top of the graph, as well as those next to the x- and y-axes. After selecting this command, specify First, Second, X-Axis, or Y-Axis. Then type the text you want to display for that title and press ENTER. Select Quit from this sticky menu to return to the main Graph menu.

# Adding a Graph Legend

When a graph contains more than one series, you'll want to use a legend in your graph to show what each series represents. For example, if you are graphing division sales for several years and each series represents a different division, you will want to name the division each series represents.

The text for the legend is added with the /Graph Options Legend command. It's simple: Select this command, specify the letter of the series for which you are adding a legend, type the legend text for the series, and press ENTER. 1-2-3 produces a legend for any series that appears in the graph and for which you have entered legend text.

---

## /Graph Options Legend

This command lets you enter text for a legend to identify each series in all graphs except pie charts. After selecting this command, choose the series for which you want the legend to appear, type the legend text, and press ENTER. Select Quit from this sticky menu to return to the main Graph menu.

---

# *Creating Your Own Graph*

Let's build a simple worksheet and then graph it in some of the graph formats.

1. Start in cell A2. Type **ABC Company** and press the DOWN ARROW.

2. Type **/WCS** to select the /Worksheet Column Set-Width command. Type **12** and press ENTER to set the new column width.

3. In A3, type **XYZ Company** and press HOME and then the RIGHT ARROW.

4. Starting in B1, type **1989** and press the RIGHT ARROW. Type **1990** and press the RIGHT ARROW. Type **1991** and press the DOWN ARROW once and the LEFT ARROW twice.

5. Starting in B2, type **350000** and press the RIGHT ARROW. Type **480000** and press the RIGHT ARROW. Type **530000** and press the DOWN ARROW once and the LEFT ARROW twice.

6. Starting in B3, type **650000** and press the RIGHT ARROW. Type **520000** and press the RIGHT ARROW. Type **470000** and press ENTER. Your worksheet entries look like what is illustrated at the top of the next page:

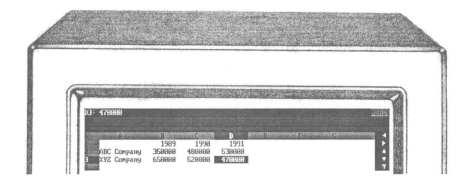

Now let's create some graphs with this data.

1. Type **/G** to display the main Graph menu.

2. Type **X** to enter values along the x-axis. Press HOME and the RIGHT ARROW, type a period, and press the RIGHT ARROW twice and ENTER once. This specifies a range that includes the years in row 1 as the labels for the x-axis.

3. Type **A** to specify the graph's first series. Press the UP ARROW, type a period, and press the LEFT ARROW twice and ENTER once to use the range B2..D2.

4. Type **B** to specify the graph's second series. Type a period and press the LEFT ARROW twice and ENTER once to use the range B3..D3.

5. Enter the graph's titles.

   a. From the main Graph menu, type **OTF** to select /Graph Options Titles First. Type **ABC Company** and press ENTER.

   b. Type **TS** to select Titles and Second, and enter **ABC Company's Market Share is Growing** for the graph's second title.

   c. Type **TY** to select Titles and Y-Axis and enter **Sales** for the Y-Axis label.

6. Enter the legend text. Type **LA** to select Legends and **A** series, type **ABC Company** for the series A legend, and press ENTER. Type **LB** and enter **XYZ Company** for the B series legend.

7. Type **Q** to return to the main Graph menu.

8. To display the worksheet data as a line graph (the default graph type), type **V** to select/Graph View. Notice how 1-2-3 has translated the data from your worksheet into the graph. When you are done, press any key to remove the graph.

9. Now let's look at a pie chart of your data. From the main Graph menu, type **TP** to select Type and Pie, and then type **V** to display the graph. Notice how the graph only includes the A series (a pie graph only uses one data series). Press any key to remove the graph.

10. Type **TB** to select Type and Bar and then type **V** to see a bar graph of your data. Press any key to remove the graph.

11. Type **Q** to select Quit and return to READY mode.

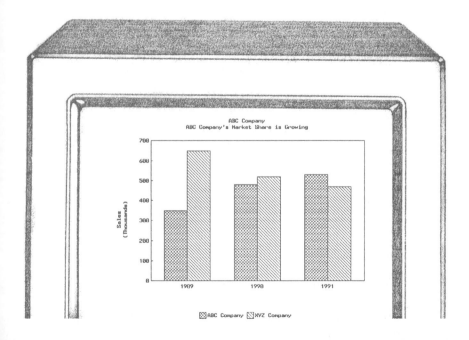

Graphs in 1-2-3 always reflect the current worksheet values, so if these values change, the graph changes, too. To test this out, move the cell pointer to D3 of the sample worksheet and change the entry there to **300000**. Press **ENTER** to replace the 1991 sales figure for the XYZ Company with this new amount. Now press **F10** (**GRAPH**) to display a graph; you'll get a bar graph since that's the current graph type (from Step 10 of the preceding procedure). Notice that the graph reflects the new sales amount that you just entered.

# Printing a Graph

The process for printing your 1-2-3 graphs varies depending on the release of 1-2-3 you are using. Releases 1A through 2.3 include a program called PrintGraph that prints your graph. In Releases 3 and 3.1, you can print graphs using 1-2-3's Print menu. Both methods require that your printer is correctly installed and capable of printing graphs (some printers cannot).

## Using PrintGraph

If you are going to print your graphs with PrintGraph, you must first perform a few steps of preparation before you can use the PrintGraph program. You need to tell 1-2-3 whether you will print the graph using available colors or in black and white, and you must save a picture of the graph in a separate file that PrintGraph can use.

### Choosing Color or B&W

If you want to print your graph using a "black-and-white" printer (that is, it prints only one color, usually black), you need to tell 1-2-3 that you want the various data series to be distinguished using hatch patterns instead of colors. This change will be apparent on your screen as well as your printer. To do this, use the **/Graph Options B&W** command. If you forget to execute this command, the data series in your graph will all look the same. You can easily return to using colors for the series by selecting /Graph Options Color.

## Saving the Graph in a .PIC File

Before printing a graph with PrintGraph, you must save a picture of the graph in a file separate from the worksheet file that contains the graph settings. To do this, select the /Graph Save command. When you are prompted for a filename, type a name with up to eight characters and press ENTER. 1-2-3

**MY_ DATA.WK1**

|   | A | B | C |   |
|---|---|---|---|---|
| 1 | ABC Company Sales | | | |
| 2 | | | | |
| 3 | | _ 1989 | 1990 | |
| 4 | Dollar Sales | 350000 | 480000 | |
| 5 | Unit Sales | 50000 | 75000 | |
| 6 | | | | |
| 7 | | | | |

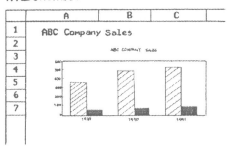

**MY_ DATA.PIC**

automatically adds a .PIC filename extension. This .PIC file is separate from the worksheet file.

Now you can save your worksheet data and exit 1-2-3 so you can use the PrintGraph program.

## /Graph Options B&W

This command tells 1-2-3 to distinguish data series in a graph using hatch patterns instead of colors. You can select /Graph Options Color to display the series in the graph using colors. You will need to select Quit to return to the main Graph menu.

## /Graph Save

This command saves the current graph in a .PIC file that other programs such as PrintGraph can use. After selecting the command, enter the filename for this graph and press ENTER.

### Running PrintGraph to Print a Graph

Once you have a graph .PIC file, you can run the PrintGraph program to print it. (You must have PrintGraph installed on your hard disk or available on a floppy disk.)

1. Save the worksheet with the current graph settings to ensure that they are available if you use the worksheet later. Use /File Save, type **GRAPH** as the filename, and press ENTER.

2. Exit 1-2-3. If you are using a floppy disk, insert the PrintGraph disk into the appropriate drive. Start PrintGraph by typing **PGRAPH** and pressing ENTER. (In Release 1A, type **Graph** and press ENTER.)

3. Tell PrintGraph which graph you want to print. Choose Image-Select (or Select in 1A). PrintGraph lists the graph .PIC files. In this list, press the UP ARROW and DOWN ARROW to highlight the graph file you want, press the SPACEBAR to mark the file, and press ENTER to return to the menu.

4. Select **Go** to print the file. If need be, respond to the prompts for inserting pens in a plotter or feeding the next sheet of paper.

5. When PrintGraph finishes, type **P** to select Page and advance the paper in the printer to the next page.

6. Finally, type **E** to select Exit to leave PrintGraph. In some instances, you may need to use other PrintGraph commands before you can print your graphs. These commands are listed in the box "Other PrintGraph Commands."

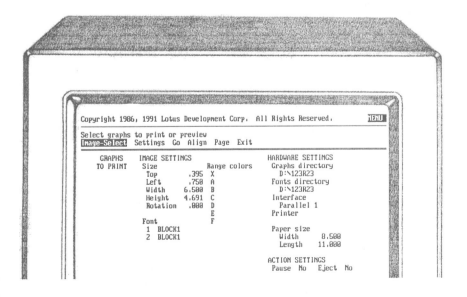

# Other PrintGraph Commands

Depending on how your PrintGraph program is set up, you may need to use one or more of these commands to print your graph:

- *Settings Hardware Graphs-Directory*    Lets you specify the directory where your graph .PIC files are located. In Release 1A, this command is **Configure Files Pictures.**

- *Settings Hardware Fonts-Directory*    Lets you specify the directory where 1-2-3's font files are stored. In Release 1A, this command is **Configure Files Fonts.**

- *Settings Hardware Printer*    Lets you select the printer (and print quality) you will use among the printers selected during installation. In Release 1A, this command is **Configure Device.**

- *Settings Image Font 1 (or 2)*    Lets you select the font the graph uses for the first title (or the other graph text). In Release 1A, this command is **Options Font 1** (or **2**).

# Using the Print Menu

In Releases 3 and 3.1, you can print a graph simply by using 1-2-3's Print menu. To tell 1-2-3 that you want to print a graph, select **/Print Printer Image.** 1-2-3 displays the word *Current* for the current worksheet graph; just highlight it and press ENTER. When you select Go, 1-2-3 prints the current graph. Printing the graph this way means you can also use other selections in the Print menu such as **Align** and **Page.**

## /Print Printer Image

In Releases 3 and 3.1, this command selects the graph 1-2-3 will print when you select /Print Printer Go. When you print a graph in this way, you can use other Print menu commands to advance the paper to the next page and start printing. After selecting this command, specify a named graph or select Current to print the graph that appears when you press **F10** (GRAPH).

# *Printing Your Sample Graph*

If you have an appropriate printer, try printing the sample graph you've been using in this chapter. Remember, the steps you'll follow depend on the 1-2-3 release you are using.

For readers using any of the 1-2-3 Releases 1A through 2.3, here is the procedure for using the PrintGraph program. Start with the sample graph displayed on the screen.

1. If your printer can only print using one color, on the main 1-2-3 menu type **/GOBQ** to select the /Graph Options B&W command and then Quit to return to the main Graph menu.

2. Save a .PIC version of the graph. Type **S** to select Save, type **MY_GRAPH** as the filename, and press ENTER. Type **Q** to return to READY mode.

3. Save the worksheet with its current graph settings. Type **/FS** to select the **/File Save** command, type **GRAPH** as the filename, and press **ENTER**.

4. Leave 1-2-3 by typing **/QY** to select the **Quit** command with a **Yes** confirmation.

5. Start PrintGraph by typing **PGRAPH** and pressing **ENTER**.

6. Type **I** to select Image-Select. Press the **DOWN ARROW** until MY_GRAPH is highlighted in the list of .PIC files. Press the **SPACEBAR** and **ENTER**.

7. Type **G** to select **Go** to print the file. Respond to PrintGraph's prompts as appropriate. When printing has finished, type **E** to select Exit and leave PrintGraph.

In Release 3 and 3.1, you can print your graph using the Print menu. Type **/PPI** to select **/Print Printer Image**. Press **ENTER** to select Current. Type **AGPQ** to select **Align**, **Go**, **Page**, and **Quit** to print the graph.

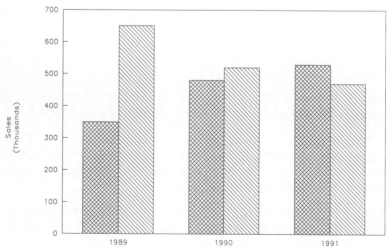

# Keys to Success

You can display your worksheet data in a graph using just a few 1-2-3 commands. Graphs provide a different and more illustrative method of presenting your numerical data to an audience. 1-2-3 lets you quickly create graphs without having to learn a special graphics software package.

Once the worksheet data to graph is on the screen, use the /Graph commands to create the graph. First, select /Graph X and specify the worksheet range to put along the x-axis. Next, select **A** through **F** for up to six data series to represent on the graph, and specify the range each series will use. Using Graph Type, choose a line, bar, pie, or stacked bar graph format. You can add explanatory text using Options Titles and choosing from four locations for this text. It's wise to identify each series in the graph with a legend, using Options Legend.

To display a graph, select View from the main Graph menu or press **F10 (GRAPH)** from the worksheet. Select Quit to return to READY mode.

Printing a graph involves a different process depending on the 1-2-3 release you have.

- If you are using PrintGraph (Releases 1A through 2.3) and your printer only prints one color, select /Graph Options B&W. Save a picture of the graph in a .PIC file by selecting /Graph Save and typing a filename. Then leave 1-2-3 (after saving the worksheet if necessary) and start PrintGraph by typing **PGRAPH** and pressing ENTER. In PrintGraph, select Image-Select, highlight the .PIC file to print, press the SPACEBAR and then ENTER. Select Go to print the file and Exit to leave PrintGraph.

- If you are using the Print menu (Releases 3 and 3.1), select /Print Printer Image, choose Current, and select Align, Go, Page, and Quit to print the current graph.

# What Do They Mean By . . . ?

**Hatch Pattern**  A pattern used to distinguish the data series in bar graphs.

**Legend**  Text under the x-axis that identifies the data series in a graph.

**Series**  A group of related worksheet values, represented by the same hatch pattern or color on the graph.

**X-axis**  The horizontal line at the bottom of a graph.

**Y-axis**  The vertical line that measures quantity and determines the height of the points in a graph.

# Using Wysiwyg Features in Releases 2.3 and 3.1

In Chapter 5, you learned how to print your worksheet data. Printed worksheets often look different from how they appear on the screen. If you use advanced 1-2-3 printing features or have your 1-2-3 reports professionally typeset, your printed data will often look dramatically different from its screen display.

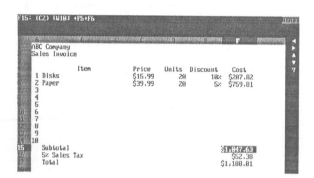

### ABC Company
#### Sales Invoice

| | Item | Price | Units | Discount | Cost |
|---|---|---|---|---|---|
| 1 | Disks | $15.99 | 20 | 10% | $287.82 |
| 2 | Paper | $39.99 | 20 | 5% | $759.81 |
| 3 | | | | | |
| 4 | | | | | |
| 5 | | | | | |
| 6 | | | | | |
| 7 | | | | | |
| 8 | | | | | |
| 9 | | | | | |
| 10 | | | | | |
| | Subtotal | | | | $1,047.63 |
| | 5% Sales Tax | | | | $52.38 |
| | Total | | | | $1,100.01 |

1-2-3 Releases 2.3 and 3.1 include a new feature called *Wysiwyg* (usually pronounced "wiz-i-wig") that adds *spreadsheet publishing* features to the 1-2-3 program. Wysiwyg means "What You See Is What You Get." With Wysiwyg, you can display the worksheet exactly as it will appear when you print it. You can also add formatting codes to the worksheet to employ printing features like boldface and italic. Wysiwyg also lets you print a graph on the same page with the worksheet data, without exiting 1-2-3.

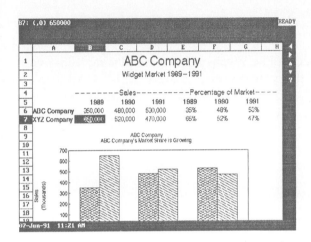

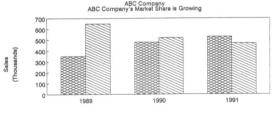

Wysiwyg is a 1-2-3 *add-in*; in order to use it, you must install it and then attach it to 1-2-3. Add-in software provides additional features not available within 1-2-3. Some add-ins are packaged (or "bound") with 1-2-3, as Wysiwyg is; other add-ins are available through separate vendors. Once the add-in is attached, its features are readily available through commands in 1-2-3.

*Note: If your monitor cannot display graphics, you can still use Wysiwyg, though the appearance of your worksheet display will differ from the printout.*

## Attaching the Wysiwyg Add-in

When you attach an add-in like Wysiwyg, you are placing it into your computer's memory so that you can use its features in 1-2-3. Add-ins are attached using the 1-2-3 Add-In menu. This menu is displayed when you press **ALT-F10 (Add-In)**. In Release 2.3, the Add-In menu looks like this:

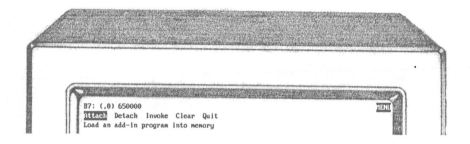

This menu looks different in Release 3.1. To attach an add-in for use with 1-2-3, use the following procedure. If you have the Wysiwyg add-in installed, this procedure shows you how to attach it. Once Wysiwyg is attached, it remains in memory until you leave 1-2-3.

1.  Save any worksheet you have on your screen and return to the 1-2-3 main menu. To display the Add-In menu, press **ALT-F10**.

2.  Type **A** to select Attach (in Release 3.1, type **L** for Load). 1-2-3 displays a list of the installed add-ins.

3.  Use the **RIGHT ARROW** to highlight the Wysiwyg add-in and press **ENTER**.

4.  You'll next see selections that you can choose for the method by which the add-in will be called up in 1-2-3. You can use the function key combinations **ALT-F7**, **ALT-F8**, **ALT-F9**, and **ALT-F10** to invoke

add-ins. To start Wysiwyg's menu, however, you will type a colon, so type **N** to select the No-Key option. Wysiwyg is now loaded, and the 1-2-3 display changes to show the worksheet as it will appear when you print it.

5. When 1-2-3 returns to the Add-In menu, type **Q** to select **Quit** to return to the READY mode.

---

# (ALT-F10) Attach (Release 2.3)
# (ALT-F10) Load (Release 3.1)

This command loads an add-in into 1-2-3. After selecting this command, choose Attach in Release 2.3 or Load in Release 3.1. Select the name of the add-in you want to attach. Next select the function key that you want to use to invoke the add-in; or select the No-Key option if the add-in does not need to be invoked or has its own start-up key combination.

---

# Worksheet Files in Wysiwyg

When you save your Wysiwyg worksheet using 1-2-3's /File Save command, Wysiwyg saves the Wysiwyg features you add to the worksheet in a separate file. This file has the same name as the worksheet, but with a .FMT (Release 2.3) or .FM3 (Release 3.1) filename extension. The next time you retrieve your worksheet in Wysiwyg, the Wysiwyg formatting information is retrieved as well. If you retrieve a worksheet without Wysiwyg loaded, you will not see the Wysiwyg formatting.

# Using Wysiwyg Commands to Format Worksheet Entries

Wysiwyg's format capabilities can give your worksheet entries character-istics that would normally require a word processing package. For ex-ample, with a word processor you can create boldface or italic text or change the appearance of the characters by assigning a different font style or size. Wysiwyg's menu includes commands for adding this type of formatting to worksheet cells.

## Using Boldface

Boldface lets you emphasize certain entries on the worksheet, such as report totals or column headings. Let's try using Wysiwyg to add boldface to a few entries in a simple worksheet.

1. Make sure Wysiwyg is installed and attached to 1-2-3.

2. On a clear worksheet screen, move to A1, type **ABC Company Sales Report** and press the DOWN ARROW. Type **Widget Sales** and press the DOWN ARROW twice. Type **Dollar Sales** and press the DOWN ARROW. Type **Unit Sales** and press ENTER.

3. Type **/WCS** to select the /Worksheet Column Set-Width command. Type **15** and press ENTER to set a new column width.

4. Press the UP ARROW twice and the RIGHT ARROW once. In cell B3, type **1989** and press the RIGHT ARROW. Type **1990** and press the RIGHT ARROW. Type **1991** and press the DOWN ARROW once and the LEFT ARROW twice.

5. In cell B4, type **350000** and press the RIGHT ARROW. Type **480000** and press the RIGHT ARROW. Type **530000** and press the DOWN ARROW once and the LEFT ARROW twice.

6. In cell B5, type **50000** and press the RIGHT ARROW. Type **75000** and press the RIGHT ARROW. Type **95000** and press ENTER. Your worksheet looks like this:

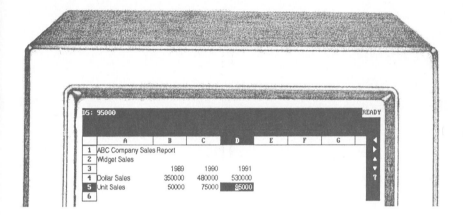

7. To add boldface to the column-head entries in B3..D3, press the UP ARROW twice and the LEFT ARROW twice to move to B3, which is the first cell you want in boldface.

8. Remember—Wysiwyg is loaded, so type a colon (:) to display Wysiwyg's main menu:

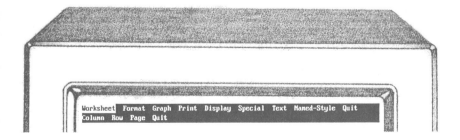

9. From this menu, type **F** to select Format, **B** to select Bold, and **S** to select Set. When Wysiwyg prompts for the range to format, press the RIGHT ARROW twice to select the range B3..D3, and press ENTER. The entries in this range now appear in boldface, as shown here:

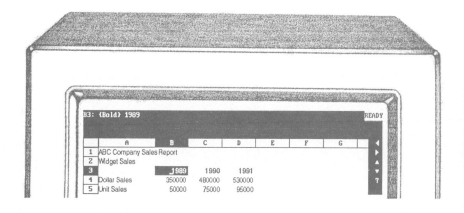

*Note:* *In the preceding illustration, notice that the control panel display for cell B3 includes the {Bold} indicator. When Wysiwyg is loaded, the control panel shows, in curly braces, any Wysiwyg formatting added to the current cell.*

If you later want to remove the formatting from any entries, use the Clear option for the appropriate Wysiwyg format command. For example, to clear the boldface formatting you just added to the ABC Company Sales Report, type **:FBC** to select Wysiwyg's **:Format Bold Clear** command, select the range from which to remove the boldface, and press ENTER.

## :Format Bold Set and
## :Format Bold Remove

These two Wysiwyg commands add and remove boldface to and from cell entries in a worksheet range. After selecting the command, specify a worksheet range and press ENTER.

## Using Different Fonts

*Fonts* are collections of typeface styles and sizes that determine the appearance of the characters in a worksheet. Wysiwyg includes four typeface styles: Swiss, Dutch, Courier, and XSymbol, all of which can display in a variety of sizes. The font sizes are measured in *points*. Points are 1/72 of an inch, so a character that is 12 points high is 1/6 of an inch tall. Wysiwyg lets you select up to eight different fonts for your worksheet entries. The easiest fonts to use are the eight default fonts provided by Wysiwyg.

Try changing some of the fonts used in your ABC Company Sales Report sample worksheet.

A B C a b c 1 2 3
*Swiss*

1. Press HOME to move to A1.

A B C a b c 1 2 3
*Dutch*

2. Type **:FF** to select Wysiwyg's :Format Font command. Wysiwyg displays a dialog box that lists the fonts you can select.

A B C a b c 1 2 3
*Courier*

②③④ ➡ ≫ ≻ ⑥⑦⑧
*XSymbol*

3. Now you need to indicate the font (a number between 1 and 8) you want to assign to a particular range. For the text in A1, type 3 to select Swiss 24 point. Now Wysiwyg wants to know the range to format in this font. Press ENTER to select A1, and 1-2-3 displays this label with the Swiss 24-point font.

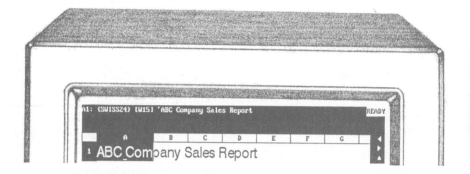

4. Try another font: Press the DOWN ARROW twice to move to A3. Type :FF6 to select Wysiwyg's :Format Font command and the Dutch 6-point font. Press the DOWN ARROW twice, the RIGHT ARROW three times, and ENTER once to select A3..D5. Now your entries look like this:

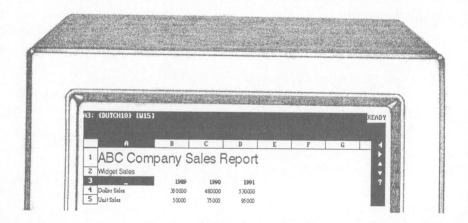

## :Format Font

This Wysiwyg command sets the font for a worksheet range. After selecting this command, type a number between 1 and 8 for the font you want to assign. Next, select a worksheet range and press ENTER.

# *Using Wysiwyg to Add a Graph to a Worksheet*

You can use Wysiwyg to display a graph in a worksheet range. This lets you combine graphs with worksheet data. The graph appears in place of a worksheet range.

## ABC Company Sales Report
Widget Sales

|             | 1989   | 1990   | 1991   |
|-------------|--------|--------|--------|
| Dollar Sales | 350000 | 480000 | 530000 |
| Unit Sales   | 50000  | 75000  | 95000  |

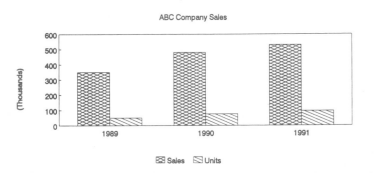

To add the current graph to a worksheet, you use the Wysiwyg :Graph **Add** Current command and specify where on the worksheet you want filled with the graph. You select this range, press ENTER, and Wysiwyg makes the graph as large as possible within the specified range.

In this next exercise you will use your practice worksheet, create a graph, and combine them.

1.  First you need to create a graph with the ABC Company Sales Report data. Press the RIGHT ARROW to move to B3. Type **/GTB** to select Graph, Type, and Bar to make a bar graph.

2.  To determine the values along the x-axis, type **X**, type a period, press the RIGHT ARROW twice, and press ENTER.

3.  To designate the graph's first series, type **A**, press the DOWN ARROW, type a period, press the RIGHT ARROW twice, and press ENTER. Then choose the graph's second series: type **B**, press the DOWN ARROW twice, type a period, press the RIGHT ARROW twice, and press ENTER.

4.  Type **OTF** to select Options, Titles, and First. Type **ABC Company Sales** and press ENTER.

5.  For the first series legend, type **LA** for Legends and series **A**, type **Sales**, and press ENTER. For the second series legend, type **LB** and **Units** and press ENTER.

6.  Type **Q** to select Quit and return to the main Graph menu. Type **V** to display the graph. Press any key to remove the graph. Type **Q** to select Quit and return to READY mode.

7.  Now you want to add the graph to the worksheet. Type **:GAC** to select Wysiwyg's Graph Add Current command. When Wysiwyg prompts for a range, type **A7..D15** and press ENTER. Wysiwyg displays the current graph in this range, as shown here:

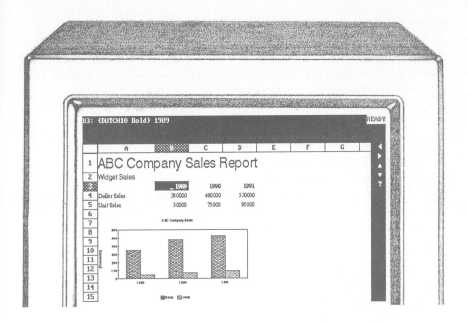

## :Graph Add Current

This Wysiwyg command displays the current graph in a worksheet range. After selecting this command, specify a worksheet range to be filled with the graph and press ENTER.

# Printing with Wysiwyg

When you've added the Wysiwyg formats you want to use in your worksheet and added graphs as needed, you can use Wysiwyg to print the worksheet with the formats and graphs you have added. A worksheet printed with Wysiwyg includes the Wysiwyg formats and graphs as long as they are part of the range you print. Remember, what you see is what you get, so printing a Wysiwyg worksheet is like cutting the worksheet out of the screen and pasting it on paper.

When you print with Wysiwyg's Print menu, you will print using Wysiwyg features. If you print with 1-2-3's Print menu, the Wysiwyg features are ignored.

Wysiwyg's Print commands are similar to 1-2-3's Print commands. Let's use them to print the worksheet you've just created.

1. Type **:P** to select the Wysiwyg **Print** command. Like printing with 1-2-3, Wysiwyg has a dialog box for choosing print options; it will appear as soon as you type **:P**. Then type **RS** to choose Range Set.

2. Select the range to print; for the worksheet you created earlier, this is A1..D15. Press ENTER.

After you select the range, Wysiwyg surrounds it with a dotted line. If the range that you are printing will be divided into multiple pages, each worksheet range that will appear on its own page will have a dotted outline around it. Since the graph was added to the worksheet, it will print along with the worksheet data when you print from Wysiwyg.

3. Type **CP** to select Config (or Configure) and Printer, highlight a printer and print quality from the list, and press ENTER. Then type **Q** for Quit to return to Wysiwyg's Print menu.

4. When you are ready to print the selected range, type **G** to select Go, and Wysiwyg will print the data and return to READY mode. Unlike printing from 1-2-3, you do not need to select Align, Page, and Quit as part of printing your worksheet.

# ABC Company Sales Report
Widget Sales

|  | 1989 | 1990 | 1991 |
| --- | --- | --- | --- |
| Dollar Sales | 350000 | 480000 | 530000 |
| Unit Sales | 50000 | 75000 | 95000 |

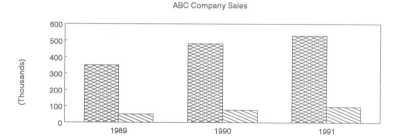

ABC Company Sales

# :Print Range Set

This Wysiwyg command lets you choose a worksheet range to print with Wysiwyg. After selecting this command, specify the range to print and press ENTER. If the worksheet range includes any displayed graphs, they will be printed.

# :Print Config Printer

This Wysiwyg command selects the installed printer and print quality for printing your worksheet range with Wysiwyg. After selecting this command, choose a printer and print quality from the list and press ENTER. Next, type **Q** for Quit to return to Wysiwyg's Print menu.

# :Print Go

This Wysiwyg command starts the printing of a worksheet range, with all of the Wysiwyg formats and graphs you have added. After printing is finished, Wysiwyg returns to the READY mode.

# Keys to Success

Wysiwyg is an add-in program that is packaged with 1-2-3 Releases 2.3 and 3.1; this program lets you add spreadsheet publishing features to your worksheet. Add-ins such as Wysiwyg enhance your use of 1-2-3 by giving you additional features to access from within the 1-2-3 program. Wysiwyg lets you format worksheet entries using attributes such as boldface and various font styles and sizes; you can also add graphs to your worksheet.

To use Wysiwyg, you must install it into your computer and then attach it to 1-2-3. To attach an add-in, select the ALT-F10 Attach command in Release 2.3 or the ALT-F10 Load command in Release 3.1. Then select Wysiwyg, No-Key, and Quit to attach Wysiwyg and return to the READY mode. With Wysiwyg attached, you can access the Wysiwyg commands by typing a colon (:).

The Wysiwyg :Format Bold Set command lets you add boldface to a range of worksheet entries. With Wysiwyg :Format Font you can assign one of eight fonts to a worksheet range. To display the current graph in a worksheet range, use Wysiwyg :Graph Add Current.

When you finish adding the Wysiwyg features to your worksheet, you can print it using Wysiwyg rather than 1-2-3 so your printed copy includes the Wysiwyg enhancements. The range to print is set with the Wysiwyg :Print Range Set command. The printer is selected with the Wysiwyg :Print Config Printer command. To start printing, select Wysiwyg :Print Go.

# What Do They Mean By . . . ?

Add-in  A separate software product that you can use within 1-2-3 to add other features.

Attaching an Add-in  Loading an add-in into memory so it is available within 1-2-3.

Font  The style and size of characters.

Points  Units of 1/72 of an inch by which Wysiwyg measures the size of worksheet characters.

# *Installing*
# *1-2-3*
# A

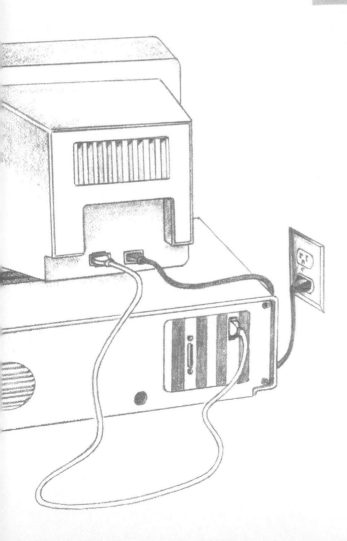

Before you can use 1-2-3, it must be installed on your computer. Installation can be as simple as creating a backup copy of the program files on floppy disks and/or copying the files to the hard disk. During the installation process you will also select the equipment you will use with 1-2-3 (display, printers, etc.). Each release of the 1-2-3 program is installed a little differently, and this appendix contains a brief description of the installation process for all but the oldest of 1-2-3 versions.

These directions assume you know how to use DOS commands such as COPY, FORMAT, and MD. If you have never used these DOS commands, you should begin by consulting a DOS reference or a book such as Osborne/ McGraw-Hill's *Simply DOS*.

# Installing Release 2.01

1-2-3 Release 2.01 can be run from floppies or a hard disk.

*To use Release 2.01 with floppy disks,* first use the DOS FORMAT command to prepare as many blank disks as you have 1-2-3 program disks. Then copy the files from the 1-2-3 disks to your newly formatted disks. You will want to copy your computer's COMMAND.COM file to your copies of the 1-2-3 disks labeled System, Backup System, A View of 1-2-3, PrintGraph, and Utility, to allow you to temporarily exit to DOS while using 1-2-3. Next, put the Install disk in drive A, type **INSTALL**, and press ENTER. Insert each of the program disks in drive A as the Install program prompts you for them. Select First-Time Installation. Specify your display type and both a text and graphics printer if you plan to print both text and graphics. You can change the name of the driver set, which defines your equipment selections to 1-2-3, if you wish. Continue replacing the disks as the installation program prompts for them. When you return to the menu, select Exit Install Program to return to DOS. To start 1-2-3, place the System disk in drive A, type **123**, and press ENTER.

*To use Release 2.01 on a hard disk,* first use the DOS MD command to create a directory for your 1-2-3 files. For example, type **MD \123** to create the 123 directory immediately beneath the root directory on the current disk drive. Use the DOS COPY command to copy the files from each of the program disks to the directory on your hard disk. For example, enter **COPY A:*.* C:\123** to copy all the files on the disk in the A drive to the new directory. Next, access the 1-2-3 directory on your hard disk. Type **INSTALL** and press ENTER. Select First-Time Installation and then specify your monitor type and text and graphics printers (if you are printing both text and graphics). If you wish, you can change the name of the driver set, which defines your equipment selections. When you return to the Install menu, select Exit Install Program to return to DOS. Next, put the PrintGraph disk in drive A, type **A:**, and press ENTER. Type **COPYON** and press ENTER. Follow the directions on the screen and replace the PrintGraph disk with the System disk when prompted. To run 1-2-3, switch to the 1-2-3 directory, type **123**, and press ENTER.

# Installing Release 2.2

1-2-3 Release 2.2 can be run from floppies or a hard disk. In either case, start by putting the System disk in drive A. Type **A:**, press ENTER, type **INIT**, and press ENTER. Follow the directions on the screen to register your name and company name and then return to DOS.

*To use Release 2.2 with floppy disks*, first use the DOS FORMAT command to format as many blank disks as you have 1-2-3 program disks. Then copy the files from the 1-2-3 disks to your newly formatted disks. Copy your computer's COMMAND.COM file to your copies of the 1-2-3 disks labeled System, PrintGraph, and Translate, to allow yourself to temporarily exit to DOS while using 1-2-3. Next, put the Install disk in drive A, type **INSTALL**, and press ENTER. Insert each of the program disks in drive A as the Install program prompts you for them. Select First-Time Installation and specify your display type and text and graphics printers if you plan to print both text and graphics. You can also change the name of the driver set, which defines your equipment selections to 1-2-3, if you wish. Now, continue replacing the disks as the Install program prompts for them. When you return to the Install menu, select Exit Install Program to return to DOS. To start 1-2-3, place the System disk in drive A, type **123**, and press ENTER.

*To use Release 2.2 on a hard disk*, first use the MD command to create a directory for your 1-2-3 files—for example, type **MD \123**. Use the DOS COPY command to copy the files from each of the 1-2-3 program disks to the 1-2-3 directory on your hard disk. For example, type **COPY A:*.* C:\123** to copy all the files from the disk in drive A to the new directory. Next, switch to the 1-2-3 directory on your hard disk. Type **INSTALL** and press ENTER. Select First-Time Installation and specify your display type and text and graphics printers if you plan to print both text and graphics. You can also change the name of the driver set, which defines your equipment selections to 1-2-3, if desired. When you return to the Install menu, select Exit Install Program to return to DOS.

The Allways program accompanies Release 2.2 of 1-2-3; to install Allways on your hard disk, put the Allways Setup disk in drive A. Type **A:**, press ENTER, type **AWSETUP**, and press ENTER. Follow the directions on the screen to specify your display type and printer. Then insert each disk into drive A as 1-2-3 prompts you for it.

You are now ready to use 1-2-3; type **123** and press ENTER.

# Installing Release 2.3

1-2-3 Release 2.3 must be installed on a hard disk.

To start, put the Install disk in drive A. Type **A:**, press ENTER, type **INSTALL**, and press ENTER. Next, register your name and company name. Then select the parts of the 1-2-3 program you want to install. Indicate where you want 1-2-3 installed and respond to any prompts 1-2-3 displays. The installation program copies all the necessary files, so you may need to switch disks if prompted to. After the Install program copies the files, you can choose Select Your Equipment and specify your display type and text and graphics printers if you plan to print both text and graphics. You can also change the name of the driver set, which defines your equipment selections to 1-2-3, if you wish. If Wysiwyg is installed, the Install program next creates the fonts Wysiwyg uses. When the fonts are generated, press ENTER to return to DOS, and you are ready to run 1-2-3.

# Installing Release 3

1-2-3 Release 3 must be installed on a hard disk on an AT or PS/2.

To start, put the Setup/Install disk in drive A. Type **A:**, press ENTER, type **INSTALL**, and press ENTER. Next, enter your name and company name. Then select the operating system and specify whether you want the translation files copied. Indicate where you want 1-2-3 installed and respond to any prompts 1-2-3 displays. The installation program copies all the necessary files, so you may need to switch disks if prompted to. After the Install program copies the files, you can choose First-Time Installation and specify your display type and printer. You can also change the name of the driver set, which defines your equipment selections to 1-2-3, if you wish. Now more files are copied to your hard disk. After the files are copied, press ENTER and select Yes to return to DOS. You are now ready to run 1-2-3.

## Installing Release 3.1

1-2-3 Release 3.1 must be installed on a hard disk on an AT or PS/2.

To start, put the Install disk in drive A. Type **A:**, press ENTER, type **INSTALL**, and press ENTER. Next, register your name and company name. Then select the operating system and specify whether you want the translation files and Wysiwyg copied. Indicate where you want 1-2-3 installed and respond to any prompts 1-2-3 displays. The installation program copies all the necessary files, so you may need to switch disks when prompted. After the Install program copies the files, you can choose First-Time Installation and specify your display type and printer. You can also change the name of the driver set, which defines your equipment selections to 1-2-3, if you wish. Now more files are copied to your hard disk. Next, from the listed selections, choose the fonts you want to build; the Install program generates any fonts Wysiwyg needs. When the fonts are created, press any key to return to DOS. You are now ready to run 1-2-3.

# Index

*H*
_____